Deconstructed faith stories are the new normal. We all know people who once seemed to be solid Christians but have walked away. Alisa's story of her own reconstructed faith is a breath of fresh air. She shares her doubts and struggles and the journey God led her on to rediscover the solid Rock on which she stands. This excellent book is full of hope and sound reasons for faith in Jesus and God's Word.

> **RANDY ALCORN,** author of *Heaven, If God Is Good,* and *Giving Is the Good Life*

Is it possible to reconstruct faith after deconstruction? Using her own season of spiritual doubt as a backdrop, Alisa Childers explores the validity of Christianity—as well as the inefficacy of progressive Christianity—with precision, insight, and intellectual integrity. *Another Gospel?* is a needed and welcome book that reveals the ways historic Christianity can stand up to our doubts, concerns, and questions.

> **MELISSA KRUGER,** director of women's initiatives for The Gospel Coalition and author of *Growing Together: Taking Mentoring beyond Small Talk and Prayer Requests*

Another Gospel? is a timely, must-read book. Through the lens of her personal journey, Alisa Childers compares and contrasts the historic Christian gospel with the progressive "gospel." Nothing is more important than accurately grasping the Good News of Christ and responding to challenges against it, which is why I am grateful for her courage and clarity.

> **SEAN McDOWELL, PhD,** associate professor at Biola University and author or coauthor of over 18 books, including *So the Next Generation Will Know*

Another Gospel? is one of the most important books of our time. It shows how progressive Christianity redefines the nature of God, the mission of Jesus, and the message of the gospel—while undermining the authority of Scripture. In these pages Alisa Childers exposes this dangerous movement and points us back to a biblical faith.

MARK MITTELBERG, bestselling author of *The Questions Christians Hope No One Will Ask (With Answers)* and *Confident Faith*

If someone shares their story of deconversion from Christianity or a revisionist approach to historic Christian teachings, they'll be celebrated as authentic and find themselves trending on social media. But what about the people who look at the same evidence and decide to go deeper in their Christian faith? What I love about this truth-centered book is that Alisa shares her powerful journey of doubt on the way to a stronger faith. Readers will resonate with her honest wrestling with hard questions while at the same growing in their confidence because the answers Alisa shares are rooted in reality and Scripture. Contrary to what you may hear, you don't need to revise or reject the gospel, the atonement of Jesus, or the Bible to find real joy, peace, and love. I hope every Christian reads *Another Gospel?* so they are not taken in by the false promises of progressive Christianity.

JONATHAN MORROW, director of student discipleship at Impact 360 Institute and author of *Questioning the Bible: 11 Major Challenges to the Bible's Authority*

Alisa Childers has been where you may be now. She was *that* Christian hanging on the brink of deconversion until she found the truth—clearly explained and thoroughly defended with the facts. In *Another Gospel?* you'll find someone who has not only shared your doubts and faced your challenges, but also who found rock-solid answers to her own legitimate questions and concerns. In a witty, winsome, yet completely transparent and authentic way, Childers offers the wisdom and insight of a person who has gone through the battle and not only survived, but won.

If you've ever wondered deep inside, *Is Christianity really true?*; if you've ever agonized, *God, are you there?*, then *Another Gospel?* will be your lifeline—and God's answer to your prayer.

GREGORY KOUKL, president of Stand to Reason and author of *Tactics* and *The Story of Reality*

I love this book! Alisa Childers takes you on a captivating journey from her unreflective conservative Christian faith to the cliff of another gospel and then back home to the true Jesus. Along the way, she deconstructs progressive Christianity with wit, insight, and easy-to-remember evidence. *Another Gospel?* will inoculate you from a temptation far more seductive than atheism. And it's an enjoyable read too!

FRANK TUREK, founder and president of CrossExamined.org and coauthor of *I Don't Have Enough Faith to Be an Atheist*

Another Gospel?

A lifelong Christian

seeks truth in response to

progressive Christianity

Alisa Childers

The Tyndale nonfiction imprint

Visit Tyndale online at tyndale.com.

Visit Tyndale Momentum online at tyndalemomentum.com.

Visit Alisa Childers at alisachilders.com.

TYNDALE, Tyndale's quill logo, *Tyndale Momentum*, and the Tyndale Momentum logo are registered trademarks of Tyndale House Ministries. Tyndale Momentum is the nonfiction imprint of Tyndale House Publishers, Carol Stream, Illinois.

Another Gospel? A Lifelong Christian Seeks Truth in Response to Progressive Christianity

Designed by Eva M. Winters

Published in association with the literary agency of William K. Jensen Literary Agency, 119 Bampton Court, Eugene, OR 97404.

For information about special discounts for bulk purchases, please contact Tyndale House Publishers at csresponse@tyndale.com, or call 1-800-323-9400.

ISBN 978-1-4964-4173-7

Printed in the United States of America

26   25   24   23   22
8

For my parents,
Chuck and Karen Girard.
Thank you for giving me
the true gospel.

Contents

Author's Note

This book contains my recollections of conversations from a class I took part in more than ten years ago. Those sessions challenged my beliefs, rocked my faith, and shook me to my core. I recognize that other class members may remember some details differently, but because our discussions guided the investigation I began after those four months of study, I thought it important to reconstruct some of the dialogue to the best of my memory. It provides context to my research and the conclusions I reached regarding historic and progressive Christianity. To support the narrative flow, I also tightened the timeline in some places.

Foreword

A friend took me and several others on a sailing trip through the beautiful British Virgin Islands. As a novice sailor, I was fascinated by the serious process of anchoring the boat at night.

We would sail into a tranquil cove and drop the anchor. In order to make doubly sure the anchor had gripped securely, someone would dive into the water and inspect it. If the anchor were at all loose, it might fail during the night when we were asleep below deck. At first, this wouldn't be a problem—the boat would basically stay where it had been left. But over the long night, the gentle current and imperceptible waves would gradually cause the boat to float away, threatening to crash it onto the nearby rocks or ground it on the sandy beach.

That imagery reminds me of the urgent purpose of this book. In Christianity, the anchor is sound biblical doctrine. What happens if it's not secure or if its line is intentionally cut? Well, says philosopher Mark Mittelberg, not much at first. For a while the faith wouldn't drift too far. Tradition and habit would keep it hovering over the same spiritual vicinity, at least for a season. But the real danger is what would inevitably happen over time: The current of the culture would cause Christianity to crash on the rocks of heresy and sink into irrelevancy.

This is the alarm Alisa Childers is sounding in this powerful and persuasive new book. In a style that's at once winsome and convicting, she exposes the false gospel that so many "progressive" Christian leaders are espousing. Their aberrant beliefs are cutting adrift the faith of too many people—even though these folks may not realize it yet. As a result, Christianity is floating toward disaster—a trend that can be reversed only by returning to the sound biblical doctrine that has historically anchored our faith.

Alisa has accomplished something profound in these pages. She manages to keep her writing deft and personal, and yet she meticulously documents her points with facts and evidence. She makes concessions where appropriate, but she fearlessly confronts the distortions and outright falsehoods that fuel so much of progressive theology. With clarity, passion, and unrelenting charm, Alisa exposes the often subtle deceptions that too many Christians have been uncritically accepting as gospel truth. Her discernment is razor-sharp, her compass is pointed unswervingly toward the real Jesus, and her conclusions are solidly supported.

It's an understatement to say this book is important. It's vital. It's the right book at the right time. In fact, it may be the most influential book you will read this year. Please study it, underline it, highlight it, talk about it with others, give copies to friends and church leaders, use it in your discussion groups, quote it on social media. Take its admonitions to heart. Let it solidify your own faith so that you can confidently point others to the unchanging gospel of redemption and hope.

In sum, do your part in securing the anchor of biblical orthodoxy once more—for the sake of a church otherwise imperiled by dangerous theological drift.

Lee Strobel

Author of *The Case for Christ*
and *In Defense of Jesus*

1

Crisis of Faith

You never know how much you really believe
anything until its truth or falsehood becomes a matter
of life and death to you.

C. S. Lewis, *A Grief Observed*

The curve of the rocking chair arm dug into my hip as I held my restless toddler, singing a hymn into the darkness—darkness so thick it felt as if it were made of physical matter, choking the cries right out of my throat as I prayed to a God I wasn't sure was even there. "God, I know you're real," I whispered. "Please let me feel your presence. Please."

Nothing.

I didn't feel even the slightest goose bump or the familiar warmth that used to signify his presence to me. Swollen in breast and belly, my pregnant body ached as my little girl scampered around my lap trying to find a place to settle. Though the words seemed stuck behind my lips, I found a way to sing them out:

Before the throne of God above;
I have a strong and perfect plea . . .

Everything hurt. But I didn't protest. I remembered the promise I'd made while in the deepest pains of labor before my daughter was born. *I will never again complain about being miserably uncomfortable*, I'd declared to myself. When you're enduring pain that profound, you would give *anything* to simply be miserably uncomfortable.

After eighteen hours of back labor and five hours of pushing, Dyllan was born in distress. She was welcomed into the world by being swept out of my arms, laid on a cold metal table, and held down as tubes were stuck down her trachea. Those tubes saved her life. But it was a vexing cure. Her birth had traumatized us both.

Even so, God's peace overwhelmed me, and when they finally laid her back in my arms, I took one look at her and *I knew*. I knew with the kind of knowing that emerges from a place so deep inside, you don't even realize it's there until you need it. I knew there was nothing I wouldn't do for her now. No mountain so towering I wouldn't climb it for her. No ocean so deep I wouldn't swim it for her. No battle so formidable I wouldn't fight it for her.

But I had no idea this would be tested so soon. As I rocked my toddler that night, I was in labor again, but this time it wasn't physical. The labor was spiritual. And it wasn't a battle I had to fight just for myself. Two souls would depend on the outcome of this particular conflict of faith.

A great High Priest whose name is love;
Who ever lives and pleads for me.

But does he?

Is God really on a mystical throne somewhere out beyond the expanses of space?

Is he even aware of me?

Is everything I've ever believed about him a lie?

What happens when we die?

My name is graven on his hands;
My name is written on his heart . . .[1]

But is it?

Is the Bible really God's Word?

Is the only identity I've ever known a complete sham?

What am I supposed to tell my children?

Is religion really just the opiate of the masses?

Does God even exist at all?

"Remember, God, when Dyllan was born? Remember the peace that came over me in a wave I couldn't control? I remember. Your peace.

"Remember New York, God? Remember that day? I needed you. I remember. I remember you cradling me with your presence as I lay in my bed, feeling like I would die."

Or was it something else? Had those just been synapses in my brain firing in response to stress or excitement, sending a cocktail of endorphins and adrenaline through my body? Is that all it ever was? Every worship service, camp meeting, and Bible study?

I believe. Help my unbelief.

It felt like I'd been plunged into a stormy ocean with waves crashing over my head. No lifeboat. No rescue in sight. In the 2000 film *The Perfect Storm*, one of the last images (spoiler alert) is of the giant ship being capsized and pushed underwater by a wave the size of a skyscraper. The tiniest form of a human head peeks above the water for a split second before disappearing into the depths.

That was me.

The Real Deal

What on earth would cause a strong and devout Christian to doubt her faith? Why would a member of the popular Christian music group ZOEgirl, which toured the world giving altar calls and inspiring many young teens to proclaim their faith and "shout it from the mountain," suddenly have doubts? We'll get to that in a bit. But first, a little background.

I was that kid. You know the one. The one who asked Jesus into her heart when she was five. The one who began studying the Bible as soon as she learned to read. The one who got up early to walk around her school and pray for revival among her peers. The one who led worship in chapel at her Christian high school and moved to New York at twenty-one to do inner city work with underprivileged kids. The one who went on every mission trip she could and who evangelized on the streets of Los Angeles and New York during the summer.

The one you would never worry about. The one you just knew would be fine. The one who would never doubt her faith.

When I was about ten years old, my mom was a volunteer at the Fred Jordan Mission in Los Angeles. She would take us with her to work the soup lines on weekends, and it was there that I watched her hug prostitutes and wrap blankets around smelly homeless guys. It was there I watched my dad, a Christian recording artist, lead worship for crowds of cold and hungry souls as they sang "Amazing Grace" at the top of their lungs.

Feeding the hungry. Clothing the naked. Loving the outcast. This is what was modeled to me as genuine Christianity. It's just what Christians did. They prayed, they read their Bibles, and they served. It wasn't perfect, but it was the real thing.

So I can't say I grew up with a blind faith. My faith was informed by witnessing the gospel in action. But it was intellectually weak and untested. I had no frame of reference or toolbox to draw from when every belief I had been so sure of was called into question. And it wasn't an atheist, secular humanist, Hindu, or Buddhist who facilitated my eventual faith crisis—it was a Christian. More specifically, it was a progressive Christian pastor.

This pastor asked me to participate in an invite-only, small, and exclusive discussion group. He told me it was a ministry training course that would result in a theological education comparable to four years in seminary. "Education" was an understatement. It was more like an upheaval. The class lasted four years. I lasted four months.

We've all heard stories of Christian kids who walk away from their faith after being challenged by skeptical professors in a college classroom. My faith was confronted in a similar way . . . but not at a university. It was challenged in the pews of a church. It was rocked by a pastor who had won my trust, respect, and loyalty. This wasn't some random weirdo I'd met during a street outreach on Hollywood Boulevard who spouted vitriol against God as I handed him a gospel tract. This was an educated, intellectual, calm, and eloquent church leader—someone who expressed love for Jesus. He was a brilliant communicator, and he had a bone to pick with Christianity.

Meeting after meeting, every precious belief I held about God, Jesus, and the Bible was placed on an intellectual chopping block and hacked to pieces. Identifying himself as a "hopeful agnostic," this pastor began examining the tenets of the faith. The Virgin Birth? Doesn't matter. The Resurrection? Probably happened, but you don't have to believe in it. The Atonement? That would be a nope. And the Bible? God forbid you believed Scripture was inerrant. He pointed out that even the high schoolers had moved beyond that primitive notion. During our discussions, many in the class dismissed "fundies" (fundamentalists) as fearful dimwits who simply followed what they were told to believe.

Sure, I'd seen some of these claims before on the cover of *Newsweek* magazine or in a television special trying to debunk Jesus on the Discovery Channel. But that was no surprise. I expected non-Christians to disbelieve. I could just close the magazine or turn off the TV and go about my day. Yet in that small discussion group, there was no escaping. It seemed I was the only one in the room who was troubled by what I was asked to respond to. But I didn't have answers. *I had never even thought of some of the questions.*

I would later learn that this dismantling of doctrinal tenets—where all the beliefs someone was raised with and had never questioned are systematically pulled apart—is something progressive Christians call deconstruction.

After four months we would part ways. The pastor and the church went on to become a "progressive Christian community." At the same time, Christians all across the country were having the same types of conversations on internet message boards, in coffee shops, and in church classrooms. They were questioning their long-held assumptions about the nature of God and the Bible, the exclusivity of Christianity, and biblical norms regarding gender and sexual orientation. These disenchanted souls found each other. They wrote blogs. They penned books. Churches began identifying as progressive and removing or editing the faith statements on their websites.

Today, many of the most popular Christian authors, bloggers, and speakers are progressive. Entire denominations are now filled with those who identify as such. Yet many other Christians sit in pews every Sunday completely unaware that their church has adopted progressive theology.

Progressive Christians tend to avoid absolutes and are typically not united around creeds or belief statements. In fact, progressive blogger John Pavlovitz wrote that in progressive Christianity, there are "no sacred cows."[2] Because of this, it might be more helpful to look for certain signs, moods, and attitudes toward God and the Bible when trying to spot it. For example, progressive Christians view the Bible as primarily a human book and emphasize personal conscience and practices rather than certainty and beliefs. They are also very open to redefining, reinterpreting, or even rejecting essential doctrines of the faith like the Virgin Birth, the deity of Jesus, and his bodily resurrection.

When progressive Christianity first entered the scene, its proponents raised some valid critiques of evangelical culture that the church needed to examine and reevaluate. But those progressives who reject essential teachings—like the physical resurrection of Jesus—can confuse unsuspecting Christians and kick the foundation out from under them.

After leaving that progressive church, I was thrust into a spiritual blackout—a foray into darkness like I'd never known. I knew *what* I believed; now I was forced to consider *why* I believed. Dog-paddling to keep my head above water in that storm-tossed ocean, I begged God for rescue: "God, I know you're there. Please send me a lifeboat."

Over the course of the next few years, God did send a lifeboat. Then another. Then another. The first one came while I was driving down the interstate fiddling with the radio in my car. I stopped when I heard a gentle, grandfatherly voice addressing one of the very claims that had been lobbed at me by the progressive pastor. What I heard took my breath away and then poured it right back into my lungs. The man on the radio, who I discovered had been recorded at a university answering questions from skeptics, systematically took down objection after objection with no fear or anger. He was kind. He was resolute. He was far more convincing and fact-based than the progressive pastor. I had been searching for truth, and on the radio that day, I found it.

In no time I was reading every apologetics and theology book I could get my hands on, and I even began auditing seminary classes. The progressive wave that slammed me against the Rock of Ages had broken apart my deeply ingrained assumptions about Jesus, God, and the Bible. But that same Rock of Ages slowly but surely began to rearrange the pieces, discarding a few and putting the right ones back where they belonged.

Stronger than Before

This, then, is my account of reconstructing my faith. Today, my Christianity doesn't look exactly like it did before. I've adjusted my beliefs on certain theological points and have become much more careful in how I interpret the Bible. I've dropped some not-so-biblical ideas that were such a part of my Christian identity that I'd never thought to question them.

But throughout this journey, I've discovered that the core historic claims of Christianity are true. I've learned that the Bible, though attacked and maligned century after century, stands tall atop the rubble of accusations that have been piled up against it. I've come to know that the Christian worldview is the only one that can sufficiently explain reality. I've rediscovered Jesus . . . the confounding preacher from Nazareth who split history in two and who kept his word to never leave me. As you follow me on this journey, I pray your faith will be strengthened too.

I'm more convinced than ever that Christianity is not based on a mystical revelation or self-inspired philosophy. It's deeply rooted in history. In fact, it is the only religious system I can think of that depends on a historical event (the resurrection of Jesus) being real—not fake—news.

When I have doubts about my faith, or deep nagging questions that keep me up at night, I don't have the luxury of finding "my truth" because I am committed to *the* truth. I want to know what is real. I want my worldview (the lens through which I see the world) to line up with reality. God either exists, or he doesn't. The Bible is his Word, or it's not. Jesus was raised from the dead, or he wasn't. Christianity is true, or it isn't. There is no "my truth" when it comes to God.

Unfortunately for many people today, determining what is true in all areas of life has become nothing more than a game of "he said, she said." For example, I just googled "health benefits of pork" (because bacon), and I discovered all kinds of fun "facts." I discovered that pork is high in protein, low in carbs, gluten-free, and contains a good balance of every essential amino acid. I also read an article that claimed pork gives you healthier skin, promotes heavy metal detox, and prevents "adult disease" (whatever that is).

Obviously, what I gleaned in a five-minute Google search is a mix of facts and fantasy. How should I wade through all the information to know which sources to trust and which "facts" to believe? Should I just pile a bunch of bacon in a bowl and call it a gluten-free salad? As much as I might want to pick and choose what to believe and allow others to do the same, it's not realistic.

If "my truth" says pork is the new kale, the consequences of that idea will bear out in reality—despite how strongly I may feel about it. My feelings about bacon won't change what it's doing to my heart, my blood pressure, and my thighs. This is why "my truth" is a myth. There is no such thing. Bacon is either good for me or it's not (or it's somewhere in between, please God!). And what I believe about it can have life or death consequences.

Likewise, as I navigated through my faith crisis, I realized that it's not enough to simply know the facts anymore . . . we have to learn how to think them through—to assess information and come to reasonable conclusions after engaging religious ideas logically and intellectually. We can't allow truth to be sacrificed on the altar of our feelings. We can't allow our fear of offending others to prevent us from warning them that they're about to step in front of a bus. Truth matters for bacon eaters, and truth matters for Christians.

Maybe you're a Christian who feels alone in your beliefs. Maybe you're a believer who has drifted into progressive Christianity without realizing it—or who is concerned that a friend or loved one is on that path. Maybe you feel frustrated when your social media news feed is flooded with articles, blogs, and videos that send red flags flying, but you can't articulate why. Maybe there's a pebble in your shoe because you've witnessed hypocrisy in your church or been a victim of spiritual abuse. Maybe you're tempted to let the wave take you under and give up on your faith altogether.

Whoever you are, it is my prayer, dear reader, that this book will be a lifeboat *for you.*

2

The Rocks in My Shoes

They had turned the way of Jesus, I felt, into the club of the Pharisees, and they didn't speak for me, even though their spokesmen dominated the dialogue night after night on cable TV. The terms "Evangelical" and even "Christian" had become like discredited brands through their energetic but misguided work.

Brian McLaren, *A New Kind of Christianity*

As a touring musician, I always dreaded festival season, which generally fell right smack in the heat of summer. During this time of year, the comforts of the tour bus—complete with a private bunk, satellite TV, and minifridge—were replaced by 6 a.m. flights, bumpy van rides, and stuffy hotel rooms. And the heat. It seemed like we were always scheduled to perform at the exact moment the afternoon sun was poised to blast center stage with the full brunt of its blazing glory. Squinting into its rays, we would sing to crowds of TobyMac fans who politely tolerated us while they waited to get their Jesus Freak on. (Our main fan base, young teenage girls, didn't tend to run the festival circuit.)

One particularly dry and sunny afternoon, I sat in the

green room against an open window overlooking the festival's main stage. I watched as a charismatic preacher finished his message and began calling for young people to trek to the front and "ask Jesus into their heart." I don't mean "charismatic" in the raising-your-hands, speaking-in-tongues sort of way. I mean it in the larger-than-life, magnetic-personality kind of way. This guy was electric. Persuasive.

"If you died tonight, do you know where you would go? Would it be heaven? Hell?" His voice boomed as he paced back and forth across the stage, hunched over the microphone with the perfect blend of urgency and excitement.

Dozens of young people began flooding the altar, which was actually just a ten-foot-wide section between the front row and the stage. The area that would later serve as a mosh pit for angsty adolescent Christian hard rock fans was now filled with quiet, sober, and completely freaked-out teens who didn't think burning in hell forever sounded like a good idea.

As the first wave of teens huddled near the front, the preacher resumed his pacing, thrusting his pointed finger toward the crowd. "This is your moment! This may be the last chance you ever get! You might leave this place and get hit by a bus, or have a heart attack. Or maybe the Rapture will happen and you'll be left behind. Come. Come now! I know there are more of you who need to get up here. We'll wait."

The music swelled, and one or two more teens got up out of their seats and walked the aisle to the cheers and applause of other Christian adults and peers.

The preacher didn't let up. "Some of you are still sitting in your seats. But you're feeling something. Something in you wants to walk down here, but there's a voice in your head telling you to stay put. That's the devil. Don't listen to him. He's a liar. Come now."

As a few more stragglers made their way to the front, the preacher led the crowd in a prayer. He invited everyone who could hear his voice to pray out loud after him. After the prayer, he directed the new converts to the side of the stage and instructed them to fill out a card. Later, the number of filled-out cards was announced to the crowd, along with something about angels in heaven having a big party. And after that? I don't know. I have no idea what happened to that group of souls. Maybe they established fellowship with other believers and began to grow in their faith. Maybe the guy with the cards worked with local churches to befriend and disciple them. Maybe they went home and never thought about their decision again.

In that moment, part of me felt happy these kids would now be going to heaven when they die. But something about it stuck in my spirit like a pebble that gets lodged in your shoe. You know it's there, but you keep on walking in hopes it'll just work itself out. I wondered if those teens really comprehended what they'd signed up for. Did they understand that they were called to deny themselves, pick up their cross, and follow Jesus? Did they know that salvation isn't some kind of metaphysical fire insurance—a one-time policy you buy to lock down your eternal destination? Did they think Christianity was something they were adding to their lives to bring them inner peace or make them happy and good? This whole experience reminded me of junior high camp.

The First Pebble

I looked forward to camp every year. I would join dozens of other preteens from my church boarding yellow school buses buzzing with the excitement of being away from our parents for a whole week. High on the sense of our own autonomy and isolated from worldly distractions like TV, radio, and annoying younger siblings, we would eagerly begin our pilgrimage to the mountains of San Bernadino, California. At camp, the unsaved got saved and the saved got their big calling.

Every night for the whole week, we would attend a very long and charismatic meeting. (This time, I mean "charismatic" in the raising-your-hands, speaking-in-tongues sort of way.) The meeting would begin with a game to warm up the teenage crowd and work up our anticipation. T-shirts were launched by caffeinated youth leaders who challenged the pubescent horde to scream louder, jump higher, and play harder. After a couple of games, we'd shout/sing our way through *Petra Praise*. Gradually, the music became quieter and the tempo slower. Now we were ready. Now the Spirit could move. After we'd sung several soft and emotion-stirring songs, one of the leaders gave a short message. He followed that with the altar call—this was the longest part of the meeting, and every night it became more intense and impassioned.

I was so excited when one of the "bad boys" who had been attending our youth group finally walked to the front. Everyone had been praying for him. In my youthful zeal and naivete, I thought his life was forever changed once he had gone forward and prayed "the prayer." (And maybe now we could get married one day.) Two weeks later, he was the same as he had been before he went to camp. He didn't care about God anymore. The "high" had worn off.

I wasn't immune to the emotional intensity of those altar calls either. I, too, had responded to one. This wasn't a call for salvation, but for a deeper and more intimate relationship with Jesus . . . a recommitment of sorts. After I went forward, I was escorted into a back room where I and several others just sat and cried for what seemed like a couple of hours. Then we were dismissed to join the rest of the campers for the evening snack bar and social time. When I got home from camp that year, I abstained from watching TV for two whole weeks. I'm not sure why I associated recommitment to Jesus with a television fast, but hey, it was the eighties, and legalism was in the air. But it did make me wonder why and how such an experience could so quickly wear off. And another pebble in my shoe was planted.

For the record, I'm not against altar calls. I know many mature Christians who once walked the aisle at a Billy Graham event or a Harvest Crusade. Whenever the gospel is preached and people respond under the conviction of the Holy Spirit, I praise God for that.

But sometimes, it seemed like a numbers game . . . or like a "get out of hell free" card. Spending a good bit of my twenties on a tour bus, I saw my fair share of altar calls. I even facilitated quite a few of them. They were always well-intentioned, but I couldn't help but wonder about the lasting effects. When I compared some of the altar calls I witnessed with what I read in the Bible, they felt like cheap knockoffs—like the fake Louis Vuitton purses you could buy for twenty dollars on Bleecker Street in New York. Were we doing it wrong? And another pebble was dropped into my shoe.

Finding Community

I suppose I had a few rocks in my shoes by the time I was invited to sing some of my new songs at a local evangelical church that met in an elementary school gymnasium. I was expecting my first baby and recording a solo album as ZOEgirl was fading into history.

I was as committed to the gospel as ever, but when I walked onto this church's stage for the first time, I sang with the resolute conviction that the church had gotten some things wrong:

> But I say can't we all get along?
> I say they will know us by our love . . .
>
> I could speak with tongues of angels
> Walk on water, touch the sky
> If I can't lend a hand to a stranger
> It's all a lie[1]

Next I sang about a girl who met Jesus in a strip club because he wasn't afraid to go anywhere to seek and save her. In my third song, I asked what would happen if all our proverbial closets opened up and the dusty skeletons we'd been hiding for so long wandered out. What if they shook hands and shared stories? Maybe we wouldn't be so quick to judge each other.

Finally I sang the complicated story of a girl who put her faith in Jesus as a young child. After her parents divorced, she compromised everything she believed because a guy came along who made all the promises her daddy-deprived heart wanted to hear. Nine months later he abandoned her, but she kept their baby because deep down she knew the child she carried was stamped with the image of God. As an old woman diagnosed with cancer, she sang as she had through every stage of her life:

> *Baptize me, wash me in Your water*
> *Let it run all over me, let me call You Father*
> *Capsize me, call me Your daughter*
> *Hold me close till I get home*
> *Never let me go*[2]

The woman in the song was a composite of people I knew in real life. Women with sketchy pasts and complicated spiritual lives. Women who had put saving faith in Jesus but didn't quite live up to the squeaky-clean Christian ideal after conversion. I wrote myself into each of their stories. My own sin and redemption history haunted every word.

When I was finished singing, I sat next to my husband in one of those tan metal folding chairs that were lined up in rows to serve as makeshift pews. I was sick to death of loud and shouty preachers, so when the pastor took the stage, I was doubtful I would get anything out of his message. But his humble and calm demeanor immediately commanded my attention. In a respectful and soft-spoken tone, he told the horrific story of a woman in another country who, as I recall, had been persecuted for her faith. I'll spare you the gory details, but his impassioned narrative made me think deeply about how I would respond in a similar situation. Would I rise from the ashes to praise God despite what I'd lost? Would I trust him in the face of that kind of pain? When the sermon was over, my husband and I looked at each other knowingly. Although we had been attending a different church at the time, we eventually joined this flock of believers more regularly.

Sunday after Sunday, the sermons were dynamic, thoughtful, and persuasive. We loved the pastor's intellectual approach and fresh insights into the Scriptures. We also loved the sense of community we found among other authentic believers in this small but growing congregation. For the first time in a long time, I genuinely looked forward to going to church. We were home.

Peculiar People

About eight months later, the pastor invited me to participate in the class that would change my life forever—the class that would, like Jacob wrestling with God, leave me walking with a limp. The class that would permanently embed the voice of a skeptic into my mind—that has to this day affected my ability to read the Bible without inner conflict.

When I first sat in a church classroom with about a dozen other people, I looked around. The church had recently finished a building project, so everything felt fresh and new. To promote a discussion-style environment, we sat behind four folding picnic tables arranged in a square so we could see one another's faces.

As I glanced at the other students, I observed hip, fresh-faced young couples sitting next to older folks with knowing eyes that emanated a calm wisdom. As a new mom with a toddler at home, most of my time was spent changing diapers and trying to keep my active and curious daughter from maiming herself on whatever death trap was masquerading as a desk lamp or glass-topped coffee table. My idea of "me time" was to spend twenty seconds daydreaming about finally putting away my maternity jeans . . . or going to the bathroom by myself. Whatever intellectual energy I had left was eaten up by internet searches on potty training and how to feed your children peanuts and shellfish without killing them. Basically, my life revolved around keeping a tiny human alive. Now as I sat in this room full of people who seemed sharp, educated, and put together, I felt awkwardly out of place.

What am I doing here? Everyone else seems so much smarter than me. I don't even have a college degree.

"You've all been invited here because, in some way, you are peculiar," the pastor announced at the beginning of the first meeting. He went on to explain that we were all "out of the box" thinkers, and this class would be a safe zone for us to process our doubts and questions. He was careful to explain that he didn't consider himself the teacher of this class. Embracing the role of facilitator, he encouraged the participants to speak our minds and bring all our thoughts and questions to the table. To help guide our discussions, we would read and discuss a new book about once every two weeks.

As I looked around at the other chosen few, I wondered why he thought I was peculiar. Maybe he could see the rocks in my shoes. Maybe it was the song about the strip club. Whatever it was, he thought I was looking to buy what he was about to sell. For a moment, I thought I might be.

Then the pastor revealed, "I would consider myself a 'hopeful agnostic.'" This was a bit startling as I didn't have much experience with agnostics. As a little girl, I asked my gymnastics coach if he knew Jesus, and he told me he was agnostic. I wasn't sure what that meant, but bless my little prepubescent heart, I thought giving him a gospel tract would cure whatever spiritual disease *that* was. But I didn't know what to make of a *pastor* identifying this way. I silently scolded my subconscious for being so judgmental and vowed to keep an open mind.

The first book our class read and discussed was Brian McLaren's *A Generous Orthodoxy*. In its pages, I encountered a complete redefinition of the word *orthodoxy*. I learned that Jesus wouldn't be caught dead identifying as a Christian if he walked the earth today. My discomfort grew with each chapter I read. Some of it resonated. I related to McLaren's criticism of historically inaccurate paintings of Jesus, a sentiment I had already written into the song about the strip club. I'm old enough to remember flannelgraphs and how my Sunday school teachers captured my attention by telling stories while placing the simple cut-out Bible characters on cloth backgrounds. McLaren writes, "Through these stories, Jesus won my heart."[3] Mine too. But most of the book just wouldn't settle in my spirit. From chapter 0 (which comes between the introduction and chapter 1), McLaren seems confused about what he believes, and he begins redefining words before he even gets to chapter 1. I secretly wondered if the pastor had assigned this reading to see how sharp his students were at spotting deception.

I remember being particularly bothered by a concept McLaren called "Seven Jesuses." He described seven versions of Jesus, each based on different denominational understandings of who Christ is. He urged the reader to celebrate them all. In enlightened bliss, the rest of the class enjoyed a collective "aha moment" as we discussed his challenge. That left me wondering what was wrong with *me*. I wasn't encouraged, enlightened, or inspired. All I cared about was the *real* Jesus—the one who is described in the Bible. I tried as hard as I could to make the seven Jesuses fit into my paradigm, but I couldn't.

Maybe I'm too judgmental.

Maybe I'm too close-minded.

Why is everyone else so excited about this?

One of the younger women in the class was a singer who asked if I would be interested in getting together to do some songwriting. "I was thinking we could write a song about the seven Jesuses," she suggested. I honestly can't remember what I said to her, but my inner monologue went something like, *I don't think you'd like the song I would write about that.*

Week after week I watched my classmates become more excited about all they were learning as I grew more and more conflicted and confused. What I was reading seemed a bit like oatmeal. It tasted good when you put on the right toppings, but at the end of the day, it was just a bowl of mush.

I wouldn't hear the term *progressive Christianity* until years later. But it was clear that this group of people wanted to "progress" beyond the Christianity they had known. They were going through what would practically become a rite of passage in this new and flourishing movement: deconstruction. In the context of faith, deconstruction is the process of systematically dissecting and often rejecting the beliefs you grew up with. Sometimes the Christian will deconstruct all the way into atheism. Some remain there, but others experience a reconstruction. But the type of faith they end up embracing almost never resembles the Christianity they formerly knew.[4] Traditional understandings of the Cross, the Bible, and the gospel get taken out with the trash.

Looking back, I believe that this class wasn't really a class. It was the progressive pastor's deconstruction, and he was attempting to take us with him. He partially succeeded. After I left the class, I was isolated and alone as the doubts he planted began to take root and grow. For a while, I didn't understand what was happening to me. I was holding on to Jesus with everything I had, while the foundation of my faith shook as if hit by a tsunami, crashing down on what I thought about church and the Bible. It became difficult to read the "Good Book" that had been painted in class as, well . . . not so good. It was hard to pray. I wouldn't have known to call it deconstruction, but as I sat on the very back row of a new church for the next year, I could do nothing but hang my head and weep.

I suppose this caused so much turmoil because I wasn't eager to deconstruct or become progressive because the Christianity I had known was deep and real and true. It wasn't soiled by legalism or hypocrisy, ravaged by abuse, or oppressed by doubt. I wanted to progress in my faith . . . in my understanding of God's Word, my ability to live it out, and my relationship with Jesus. But I didn't want to progress beyond truth. Once I was put through my own type of deconstruction, I wanted to reconstruct my faith by planting my flag on the firm bedrock of truth. I *needed* to know what was true.

After I left the class and spent some time in a fog of confusion, I had an idea. Rather than redefine or reject Christianity, why not go back to the beginning and find out what the *real thing* is? Maybe the only version I knew was true . . . maybe it was false.

At the time, I didn't know where this would lead. Was

much of what I believed a farce? Were we all just singing hymns into the darkness, oblivious to living in a universe with no grand design or purpose? Or would I rediscover the foundation of truth I'd sensed so strongly in the Scriptures when I was younger? Either way, I needed to know the truth.

3

Creeds, Cobbler, and Walter Bauer

*For hundreds of years after the death of Jesus, groups
adopted radically conflicting writings about the
details of his life and the meaning of his ministry, and
murdered those who disagreed. . . . There were no
universally accepted manuscripts that set out what it
meant to be a Christian, so most sects had their own
gospels. . . . Christianity was in chaos in its early days,
with some sects declaring the others heretics.*

Kurt Eichenwald, *Newsweek*

Until I began attending the class at church, I assumed that
the word *Christianity* meant something . . . that there was
a universal understanding of what Christians believe. I pre-
sumed that these beliefs were based on what Jesus taught and
what his apostles recorded in the New Testament. And like
most people, I assumed that the stream of Christianity I was
raised in was the one that had gotten all the details right.
It's not like I thought everyone else was a heretic, but I felt
a sense of pity for the Baptists who didn't speak in tongues
or raise their hands when they sang. I gave a little side-eye
to the Presbyterians who baptized infants. Despite our disagreements over certain theological issues, I knew these other
Christians were my brothers and sisters. How did I know

this? We all believed the same core principles, whether or not we agreed on how physically enthusiastic our worship should be or how we were to baptize someone.

Now, however, I'd been blindsided by the discovery that people I worshiped with every week had vastly different views on what I assumed were nonnegotiables of the Christian faith. It was disorienting to learn that this didn't really seem to bother them. Once during a choir rehearsal for a night of worship, one of my fellow classmates stood next to me on the riser and giggled. "It's funny that we're all singing these songs and none of us have any idea what we believe!" she said. I was a bit stunned by her assumption. I knew what I believed . . . but the precious confidence I'd always had in the gospel was being confronted and dismantled by the progressive pastor and my classmates. What she found oddly amusing, I found disconcerting.

A Faith Worth Dying For

After I decided to leave the class and my husband and I left the progressive church, I found myself trying to get back to the roots of my faith. I began to devour everything I could find about Christianity in its earliest form. I wanted to understand what those people who witnessed the life and death of Jesus actually believed. I had never really thought about the fact that the first Christians didn't have an embossed leather Bible, including the New Testament, sitting in their laps when they gathered for worship like many of us do today. In fact, Paul's letters weren't even written until about twenty years or so after Jesus' death and resurrection. So I wondered, *How did people understand their faith and identify with one another?* I learned that creeds became an important form of communication to keep those first-century believers on the same page. But these belief statements weren't simply a list of doctrines Christians had to affirm to be "in." These were the convictions they lived and died for.

When Christians today think of creeds, we tend to think of the Nicene or Apostles' Creed, shared by Protestants and Catholics alike. But many Christians are unaware that our New Testament contains dozens of creeds that are hundreds of years older than their more famous counterparts. Some early Christians were literate, others were not. Creeds were an easy way to summarize and memorize their essential beliefs.

The earliest creed in the history of Christianity is probably the one found in 1 Corinthians 15:3-5. Most scholars, even liberal and skeptical ones, say that this creed first began circulating as early as two to seven years after Jesus' resurrection.[1] At first I didn't understand how certain parts of Paul's early letters could be identified as early statements of belief when his first letters weren't written until a couple of decades after Jesus' life. Then I learned how ancient creeds worked, and it reminded me of my grandmother's peach cobbler.

My grandmother, whom we affectionately called Nana, was an accomplished pie baker who lived in Bakersfield (no pun intended), California. This was about an hour and a half drive from my childhood home in the San Fernando Valley, a suburb of Los Angeles.

I always looked forward to trips to Nana's house. As a

young teen, I got to spend the night with her all by myself, which was a big deal when you grow up in a house with three siblings. At one of my sleepovers, I asked Nana to teach me how to make her famous peach cobbler. She said, "I'll teach you the easy version. It's my 'cuppa cuppa cuppa' recipe." I expected her to turn to the drawer in her kitchen that held crocheted pot holders and handwritten recipe cards. Instead, she recited the ingredients off the top of her head. "It's a cup of self-rising flour, a cup of sugar, and a cup of canned peaches with the juice." That was it—except, of course, for the whole stick of butter that she cut up and put on top. The cobbler was then baked to perfection and served warm with ice cream. To this day I have never forgotten the recipe. Why? Because it was so simple and easy to commit to memory.

Imagine I decide to write a cookbook now. In it, I include the recipe Nana recited to me in 1989. My cookbook will have been written about three decades later, but the recipe *contained within it* will be the one I was given in 1989. In other words, the recipe will be written down over thirty years after it was first passed down. That's exactly what we're looking at with the creeds recorded in the New Testament—minus the ice cream.

Back to 1 Corinthians 15:3-5. In this passage, Paul, an educated Jew, writes,

> For I delivered to you as of first importance what
> I also received: that Christ died for our sins in
> accordance with the Scriptures, that he was buried,
> that he was raised on the third day in accordance

with the Scriptures, and that he appeared to Cephas,
then to the twelve.

While scholars can spot creeds in the New Testament
writings by analyzing syntax, linguistics, and other hints in
the text, the easiest way to detect one is when the writer himself tells you what he's doing. In Jewish culture, phrases like
"delivered to you" and "having received" were ancient slang
for "Hey . . . I'm about to tell you something I didn't think up
myself. I got it from someone else who got it from someone
else."[2] This was a common way for teachers to pass traditions
down to their students, just as Paul did in the passage above.

Paul begins this passage by emphasizing that he is writing to the Corinthians about what is of *first importance*. He
is basically saying, "Buckle up, guys. Pay attention. There's
nothing more important for your faith than what I'm about
to say."

Skeptical New Testament scholar Bart Ehrman writes that
this creed "encapsulated the Christian faith, putting it all in
a nutshell."[3]

What did the earliest Christians believe? Let's break it
down.

1. *They believed that Jesus died for their sins.* Within two or
   three years of Jesus' death, Christians were affirming
   the Atonement. At the core, they believed Jesus had
   died to save them from their sins—that he died in their
   place. He wasn't simply killed by an angry mob for
   speaking truth to power. Since the Atonement is one of

the foundational beliefs of Christianity, we must think about what we mean when we say, "Jesus died for my sins." To get this question wrong is to get Christianity wrong. We'll dive deeper into this in chapter 11.

2. *They believed that Jesus was buried and raised from the dead.* Without the resurrection of Jesus, you don't have Christianity. It's that simple. Paul says it plainly later in the same chapter, when he connects the Resurrection with the Atonement. He writes, "If Christ has not been raised, your faith is futile and you are still in your sins" (1 Corinthians 15:17). In other words, if the Resurrection is not an actual event in history— if Jesus is still in the tomb—then it doesn't matter whether he died for your sins. Christianity is false. Might as well pack it up and call it a day. And since Jesus predicted his resurrection, it would make him a liar if it didn't happen, and not the sinless Messiah Christians have long believed in.

3. *They believed that Jesus' atoning death, burial, and resurrection were inseparable from the Scriptures.* Essential to early Christianity was a belief that the Jewish Scriptures were the Word of God. It's popular in some circles to say that the first Christians didn't have a Bible, but this is simply not true. They had what we now call the Old Testament, and their core beliefs were supported by and affirmed in those writings.[4] They also had the "the apostles' teaching" (Acts 2:42), which provided

the very insights that would eventually be written down in our New Testament. Interestingly, this creed mentions "in accordance with the Scriptures" twice—once in support of Jesus' atoning death and once more in support of his resurrection.

4. *They believed that their core belief in the Resurrection could be verified by evidence.* This wasn't some kind of "What does Jesus mean to you?" mushy oatmeal faith. It wasn't based on a guru sitting under a tree, receiving some cosmic revelation, and then convincing a bunch of people to buy in. It centered on history and the evidence of eyewitnesses to an event—the Resurrection. The creed mentions twelve of these eyewitnesses, and in the very next verse, Paul refers to hundreds more: "Then [Jesus] appeared to more than five hundred brothers at one time, most of whom are still alive, though some have fallen asleep. Then he appeared to James, then to all the apostles. Last of all, as to one untimely born, he appeared also to me" (1 Corinthians 15:6-8). Get this—Paul wrote this when most of those witnesses were still living. They were alive and kicking with the opportunity to say, "Hey, you're making that up. I saw no such thing." But they didn't say that. We have no record of any of the five hundred witnesses ever challenging that testimony. Finally, Paul added himself to the list of those who'd seen the resurrected Jesus (see Acts 9:3-7).

Historian and philosopher Gary Habermas notes that several other early creeds affirm the deity of Jesus.[5] Think about that. The people who saw Jesus walk this earth, heard him speak, and followed him on those dusty Roman roads in Israel also thought it was essential to confess that Jesus was God. Even ancient non-Christian history falls in line with this. A Roman magistrate and influential lawyer named Pliny the Younger who lived at the turn of the first century wrote that Christians sang hymns to Christ "as to a god."[6] In fact, Jesus actually claimed to be God himself on more than one occasion, according to the Gospels.

The most striking example is in John 8, when Jesus gets into a heated argument with some Judeans. After accusing him of being demon-possessed, they brashly ask, "Who do you think you are?"[7] Jesus is happy to answer: "Before Abraham was, I AM."[8] To modern ears, this may sound like no big deal. "I am" . . . what exactly? But to the Jews who remembered the story of their ancestor Moses meeting God—who happened to go by the name "I AM"[9]—in a burning bush, this statement was heresy. In essence, Jesus was saying, "Remember Moses? Yeah, that was me in that bush." They knew he was claiming to be God. That was blasphemy, and according to Jewish law, they could execute him for it. And they picked up stones to do just that.

Class Notes

"Has anyone read some of the gnostic writings? I really like the Gospel of Thomas," someone mentioned in class one day.

Excuse me . . . the gospel of who?, my inner monologue blared as the class began to discuss all the edgy and cool ideas they'd found in these noncanonical Gospels about Jesus. (As the months went by, I would have many angsty internal conversations like this with myself while everyone else blissfully—and recklessly?—discussed all the new, fun, provocative, exciting, and interesting ideas they had about the flaws of Christianity.)

Until that moment, I didn't know other Gospel accounts of the life of Jesus existed. "Gnostic Jesus" certainly wasn't someone my teachers made flannelgraphs about in Sunday school. I'd been a Christian my entire life . . . why was this news to me? When I got home that evening, the first thing I did was google "gnostic Gospels," and I discovered that I could read them all for free online. I started with the Gospel of Thomas. Even without having any formal apologetics or theological training, I immediately recognized a *very different Jesus* from the one I had gotten to know in Matthew, Mark, Luke, and John. This man said a few things that resembled the Jesus I knew, but much of what he said made him sound more like a capricious snake-oil salesman quoting Deepak Chopra than the sovereign King of creation. For example, the Gospel of Thomas describes a Jesus who says that it's a sin to fast, pray, and give to charity. He claims people are saved by discovering knowledge, and that the only way a woman could get to heaven is by transforming herself into a male spirit.[10] Not only was this a different Jesus, but this counterfeit Messiah was preaching a divergent gospel from the one Jesus of Nazareth taught in the New Testament accounts.

As I began to look into these "other" Gospels, I learned that many people think early Christianity was actually quite diverse—that there were many different sects that held contradictory beliefs about who Jesus was, as well as the meaning of salvation and other important Christian doctrines. In other words, they argue that there is no such thing as "historic Christianity." Instead, there were many versions of Christianity all competing for the honor of being regarded as the real thing. According to this theory, what we now call the New Testament is simply a compilation of the books that were picked by the theological "winners." As the definers of orthodoxy, they labeled all the other groups as heretics and called it a day.

For someone like me who had based her entire life on the Bible, this idea was incredibly troubling. I had to get to the truth behind it.

While studying apologetics a few years later, I learned that a German theologian named Dr. Walter Bauer first proposed this idea in a book he wrote in 1934. His theory didn't gain much momentum until the book was translated into English in 1971 as *Orthodoxy and Heresy in Earliest Christianity*. This created quite a paradigm shift in the academic world and has become popularized in more recent times by Dr. Bart Ehrman.[11] One day while trying to discover more about Bauer's hypothesis, I came across the book *The Heresy of Orthodoxy: How Contemporary Culture's Fascination with Diversity Has Reshaped Our Understanding of Early Christianity*, cowritten by New Testament scholars Michael Kruger and Andreas Köstenberger. This book offers a thorough rebuttal of the "Bauer hypothesis."

I'll give you my best (nonscholar) summation. Bauer argued that we can't claim the New Testament contains the right books because all of these competing sects of Christianity would have had their own books that simply didn't make the cut. But his argument falls apart once you study the process of how we ended up with the books we call the New Testament today. In my quest to discover historic Christianity, this is a subject I spent countless hours researching and investigating because my life had been built upon this book. Contrary to popular belief (often repeated since *The Da Vinci Code*), the books of the New Testament weren't simply "chosen" in the fourth or fifth century. The councils that met to formalize the canon were doing just that—they affirmed the books that had always been recognized as undisputed: the four Gospels, Acts, and the letters of Paul. They then settled disputes over books like James, Jude, 2 Peter, and 2 and 3 John.

In fact, Kruger and Köstenberger demonstrate that the core canon was established as Scripture among Christians by the end of the first century.[12] This is such a powerful point because these supposed "other" Gospels weren't written until the second and third centuries.[13] How could the later books compete with the four Gospels if those other books didn't even exist yet?

A couple of years after I started studying apologetics, I was listening to the *CrossExamined* radio show with Frank Turek while washing dishes one day. He was interviewing a guest who caught my attention because he was not your typical apologist. J. Warner Wallace is a highly respected Los Angeles

County detective who's been featured several times on NBC's *Dateline* because of his success in solving cold cases. As a detective he knows a thing or two about evidence. So when he began talking about evidence for Christianity, I set the soapy plate I was holding back in the sink and turned off the faucet so I could listen closely. I learned that he was once an ardent atheist before realizing he had rejected Christianity without even evaluating the evidence for or against it. Using the tools and methods that made him so successful in solving crimes, he decided to treat Christianity like one of his cold cases.

During his initial investigation, he saw a book at a local bookstore called *The Lost Books of the Bible*. As a good detective wanting to analyze every bit of evidence he could get his hands on, he was curious and bought the book. In a recent blog post, he wrote,

> I was disappointed to discover that the book should have been titled, *The Well Known, Late Lies About Jesus That Were Ignored By Christians Who Knew Better*. These texts were never part of the New Testament canon. They were written late in history and rejected by everyone who knew the truth about Jesus of Nazareth.[14]

The Bible itself demonstrates that the earliest Christians knew the difference between books that were considered Scripture and books that were not. Even though the gnostic Gospels didn't even exist yet, almost as soon as the New

Testament Gospels and the letters of Paul were written, early Christians put them on the same level as the Old Testament Scriptures. I was absolutely astonished when I learned that within the New Testament itself we find Paul quoting Luke's Gospel and calling it "Scripture" (1 Timothy 5:18). Likewise, Peter refers to "all [of Paul's] letters" as Scripture (2 Peter 3:15-16).[15] That's as early as it gets, folks.

The best evidence points to these "lost books" being the late inventions of people who weren't even alive during Jesus' ministry. On the contrary, the New Testament documents were written by actual eyewitnesses (or careful historians who interviewed the eyewitnesses) who walked with Jesus, talked with Jesus, and were commissioned by Jesus to write Christian Scripture. More on this in chapter 8.

Historic Christianity

As my deep-seated beliefs were regularly being challenged by the progressive pastor and my classmates, I found myself trying to get back to the roots of our faith—to what I call historic Christianity. Why did I choose the word *historic* rather than *traditional* or *conservative*? It's probably because those words carry too much baggage. They can mean very different things to different people. I call it "historic" because that's exactly what it is. Between the pre–New Testament creeds and the New Testament documents themselves, we have the original beliefs that defined Christianity and made it unique in the world. Sure, things went haywire from there. Even in the first century, heresies and false versions of Christianity began finding their way into the communities of believers who claimed the name of Christ. But if we look at church history as a whole, every reformation was an attempt to get back to the earliest, most biblical, and most authentic version of Christianity. I think it's time for another reformation. Not a reformation that progresses beyond historic Christianity. Not one that looks down on these early believers as less enlightened and more primitive in their understanding of God, but one that rediscovers the very definition of Christianity.

Have these core teachings been abused at some point in history? Of course.

Have they been twisted and used for evil instead of good? Absolutely.

Have they ever been traded for political power and personal gain? Yes and yes.

But as the saying goes, you can't judge a belief system by its abuses. Historically, Christians have believed that the Bible is the Word of God and that Jesus is God incarnate who died for our sins and was raised to life for our salvation. There is one thing we can be certain of: The earliest Christians—the ones who knew Jesus personally, who saw him with their own eyes and touched him with their own hands—believed the teachings laid out in the earliest creeds and New Testament writings. These aren't just modern opinions or the privileged musings of an enlightened Western civilization.

There is so much more that defines Christianity, but this is where it starts. It's so much more than this—but it can't be any less. Now that I had identified the foundation of historic Christianity, I at least had a starting point. In my view, it should be up to Jesus and the apostles to define what Christianity is.

Interestingly, many progressive Christians use liturgies and recite the Apostles' and Nicene Creeds out of respect for tradition, but often they are reinterpreting what some of the doctrines and words mean. For instance, Nadia Bolz-Weber, founding pastor of the House for All Sinners and Saints, writes about how her church employs liturgy, Scripture reading, the Eucharist, baptism, and hymns in worship.[16] Yet in an interview with the *Houston Chronicle*, she said that even though she believes in the Trinity, the Incarnation, and miracles, she's not interested in "whether every single bit of it is a fact or not."[17] At our progressive church, we regularly recited the creeds even though our pastor and many of my classmates admitted they didn't believe everything in them.

Furthermore, I had begun to notice that when members of my class at church critiqued Christianity's core beliefs, they often spent less time poring over the Scriptures to discuss the finer points of theology and doctrine and more time reflecting on their disillusionment over unanswered prayers or their personal experiences growing up in legalistic churches. At times, I related with them. Yet I couldn't help but wonder if their angst wasn't directed at the wrong target—much like the faultless peach that once received the full impact of my nephew's rage.

4

Fixing What Isn't Broken

*PTCS [post-traumatic church syndrome] presents
as a severe, negative—almost allergic—reaction to
inflexible doctrine, outright abuse of spiritual power,
dogma and (often) praise bands and preachers. Internal
symptoms include but are not limited to: withdrawal
from all things religious, failure to believe in anything,
depression, anxiety, anger, grief, loss of identity, despair,
moral confusion, and, most notably, the loss of desire/
inability to darken the door of a place of worship.*

Reba Riley

"STUPID PEACH!"

My ten-year-old nephew, Matt, screamed at the ripe, juicy
peach he held in his right hand, squished it, and chucked it
through the open front door like it was on fire. What had
this innocent little peach done to deserve such treatment?
Rewind to seconds before the fruit-smashing incident. Matt
had smacked his head on the corner of the kitchen cabinet
while grabbing the poor thing out of the fruit bowl on his
way outside to play with friends.

It wasn't the peach's fault. But right then Matt had a
choice to make. Something had to be punished. Something
or someone had to absorb the full brunt of his fury. Maybe
the cabinet was too formidable an opponent. Maybe he

feared injury or, even worse, what his mother would do should he punch or kick it. Maybe it seemed as if no one would miss one insignificant peach. Maybe he was simply reacting in blind rage against whatever was closest to him. No matter what he was thinking, the juice and pulp now running down his arm made it clear—the peach had received the due penalty.

As I became more familiar with the claims of progressive Christianity, it became clear why it was gaining so much ground. Several common themes began to emerge in our assigned books and in the conversations between our progressive pastor and my fellow classmates. Eventually I recognized that, like the peach in my nephew's scenario, they were blaming the teachings of historic Christianity for real or perceived wrongs. As a result, they were ready to chuck the whole thing and trade it in for a new set of beliefs.

It's a fact that some people have been mistreated, enduring abuse or bullying at their conservative churches. Other people have experienced honest doubts and been shut down with statements like "We don't ask those questions here." For still others, the demands and tenets of historic Christianity have become too heavy to bear in a culture that vilifies anyone who challenges social norms or whose worldview doesn't align with the wider society's. And for some, it has everything to do with the Bible. They've become convinced that the book they were taught was God's very Word reads more like a script for a horror movie than the "Good Book" they are supposed to revere and obey. Still others have encountered skeptical claims they never came across in the sheltered

Christian bubble they grew up in, while some people struggle with believing God is good when life sometimes is not.

Abuse of Power

It seems as if every time I've turned on my computer in the last few years, I've come across a new scandal in the church. From the uncovering of sexual abuse to financial misconduct to pastors who wield their power and use their pulpits to bully those in their care, there seems to be no end to the uncovering of hypocrisy.

A good friend of mine recently went through an ordeal at her church of over two decades that can accurately be summed up with one word: *abuse*. I walked with her. I watched her being tossed up and down, to and fro on the waves of doubt, forgiveness, introspection, self-questioning, and attempts to reconcile before finally embracing the truth. The pastor she had trusted and served alongside all those years had been deeply offended when she expressed a theological concern. By his own admission, his reputation mattered greatly to him, and he gave her an ultimatum—trust him unquestioningly or leave. Her husband was on staff at the church, which made her situation even harder. As they struggled to decide what to do, she was gaslighted, slandered, and shown the door without even a goodbye. Nothing had changed for the pastor, but *her* life—her faith, finances, and family relationships—had been completely upended.

Thankfully, she was able to hold on to her Christian faith. She was deeply rooted in the gospel. She had studied apologetics, the nature of truth, and biblical interpretation before this life-altering event overwhelmed her. Jesus saved her, and he used apologetics to do it. But others haven't been so fortunate.

Without most of us even realizing it, much of the current evangelical culture has become a cult of personality. As human beings, we tend to put people on pedestals . . . especially pastors. We love strength. We are drawn to power. We innately want to follow the guy who will stand up for the truth and say what needs to be said, no matter the cost. "He may be harsh, but he speaks the truth." "He doesn't mince words." "He has some rough edges . . . but so did Peter." These are all excuses people use to explain away the unbiblical and unethical behavior of some beloved church leaders. These rationalizations send wounded sheep into the arms of progressive Christianity, where they will be validated and accepted. But ultimately they will be *left to bleed out*, like someone who goes to the doctor to be treated for a flesh wound, only to be given a hug and some comforting words rather than stitches and antibiotics. It might feel nice at first, but with no real cure, the patient could lose too much blood, or the wound could fester and become infected.

And the hurt goes so deep that some resolve to leave the church completely behind. It reminds me of the time I noticed what I thought was a spider bite on my leg. I hate going to the doctor, but when the sore grew to the size of a saucer and I couldn't sleep because of the pain, I finally caved and went to the local walk-in clinic. The nurse took one look at my oozing abscess and said, "Oh, honey, that's not a spider bite."

It turns out I had contracted MRSA, or methicillin-resistant *Staphylococcus aureus*. This nasty staph infection, I learned, doesn't respond to common antibiotics. A type of superbug, it can present as an angry boil on the skin that, if left untreated, can grow deeper into the body, eventually infecting organs, blood, and bones. Not something you want to mess with!

I can't tell you how thankful I was that my medical team understood MRSA and knew how to treat it. (I did that thing you're not supposed to do and googled what happens if you don't treat MRSA. I had to close my computer when I got to the myriad of articles about amputation.) Turns out, MRSA is often remedied with the same medicine used to treat typhoid fever.

Now imagine that prior to contracting MRSA, I'd had a really bad experience with a doctor. Let's even say that this particular doctor was abusive to me. My hesitancy to step foot in another hospital would be completely understandable. However, it wouldn't change the fact that *I still needed the correct medicine to treat the MRSA.* How much worse would my problem become if I found a community of people who affirmed my feelings, gave me painkillers and a comfy bed to rest in—all while denying the true source of the problem? This would actually kill me rather than save me.

I had a MRSA problem, and the human race has a problem too . . . a sin problem. There is only one cure, and sadly, many Christians throw away the cure because of a bad church experience.

No Safe Place to Doubt

Other people leave their churches because of the way their honest doubts have been dismissed. Fuller Youth Institute (FYI) studied the spiritual progression of five hundred youth group graduates during their first three years of college. Kara Powell, FYI's executive director, wrote that one of the main reasons Christian youth abandoned their faith after high school was because, at some point in their lives, they'd expressed doubts about what they'd been taught to believe. Instead of providing a safe place to process those uncertainties, well-meaning church leaders told them they shouldn't even ask such questions in the first place. This led them to conclude that Christianity was a house of cards—the church couldn't deal with their doubts, and neither could God.[1] Sadly, this research is backed up by story after story of Christians abandoning the faith they grew up with and embracing atheism, agnosticism, or some type of progressive Christianity instead.[2]

Experiencing doubt can be incredibly scary—especially for Christians who grew up in an environment in which faith was understood to suggest *absolute certainty*. The message was clear: If you have doubts, it means that your faith is weak or that there is something wrong with you spiritually. In his book *Authentically Emergent: In Search of a Truly Progressive Christianity*, Dr. R. Scott Smith wrote, "In effect, we tell people to shut up, just take *the* biblical teaching (which, on some topics, *may* really just be our own strongly held opinions) at face value as fact and accept it *by faith*, as though that by itself is a virtue. But biblical faith is not a blind leap; it involves knowledge—that God has spoken and is trustworthy."[3] False definitions of faith that are so often taught are based on a misunderstanding of the difference between *unbelief* and *doubt*. They are not the same thing. Unbelief is a decision of the will, but doubt tends to bubble up within the context of faith.

Unbelief runs contrary to the way God created the universe. In Romans 1, Paul tells us that God has revealed himself to every person who has ever lived: "What can be known about God is plain. . . . For his invisible attributes, namely, his eternal power and divine nature, have been clearly perceived, ever since the creation of the world, in the things that have been made." So every person who has ever lived not only has knowledge of God's existence but also of his nature and some of his attributes. As a result, we "are without excuse" (Romans 1:19-20). In fact, Paul says that to disbelieve God is to actually "suppress the truth" (verse 18). Unbelief is a conscious choice to live as if God does not exist—and it's born out of sinful desires.

Doubt, however, is *an entirely different concept*. To understand doubt, it's essential to understand faith. Atheists (and sadly, many Christians) believe that faith is a blind leap in the dark—some kind of willful belief despite a lack of evidence to back it up. Many Christians have also grown up being told that faith is being 100 percent certain that Christianity is true.

I suppose I believed this too. No one explicitly taught me this, but somewhere along the way I picked up these assumptions. Yet neither is a biblical definition of faith—and both are a surefire setup for a spiritual crisis. One day in class the pastor admitted that in any given moment, he was only 60 to 80 percent certain about Christianity. At first I didn't believe him. *How can a committed Christian, let alone a pastor, be only 60 percent sure? Is this what a "hopeful agnostic" looks like?* Then he asked the rest of the class, "How many of you are 100 percent certain?" I raised my hand, expecting many others to do the same, but there were only two of us. As I glanced around the room, I understood for a moment what a zoo animal must feel like on a busy Saturday in June. My eyes were met with furrowed brows of puzzled contemplation and looks of wide-eyed wonder. If I'm honest, I don't think I really knew how certain I was. I knew I was supposed to be. I thought I was. But I had a faulty definition of faith. I would later learn that biblical faith is *trust*—and that trust is based on good evidence.

When I was a kid, I loved roller coasters. I couldn't find one fast enough, scary enough, or high enough to keep me from riding it. My parents seemed to think it was safe, so I had no reason to question it. Now, as an adult, I find myself a bit more hesitant when I fasten myself into a potential death trap looping around a track at ninety miles per hour. After all, I've heard tales of people plummeting to their deaths on such amusements. I find myself wondering, *Will this car detach from the rails and crash on top of me when it hits the ground? When was the last time a mechanic checked all these bolts and screws? Is this the fatal ride that will plaster my face all over the evening news?* In other words, age, experience, and a bit of disillusionment have caused me to *doubt* the safety of the roller coasters I once rode with reckless abandon. *But that doesn't keep me from riding them.* Even in the presence of doubt, I trust that the roller coaster will bring me back to the platform safely. If I asked for evidence to back up this trust, a park employee might let me know that the roller coasters are inspected daily by professionals who check the track for debris, cracks, and chain tension. They might assure me that the vehicles, brakes, wheels, restraint system, safety cables, and emergency stop mechanisms are all meticulously investigated for abnormalities. They might inform me that the technicians X-ray the tracks once a year to check high stress areas on the metal framework. Given this information, it would be completely reasonable to trust the safety of the roller coaster. It's not a blind leap in the dark, and it's not 100 percent certainty. It is trust based on evidence.

In a way, that's how biblical faith works. When we were kids, we naturally adopted the worldview of our parents. If we grew up in church, we likely assumed Christianity was true and would defend that belief to our friends if they disagreed. But then we grew up. We were exposed to other religious and philosophical views. Like the adult who begins to doubt the safety of roller coasters, we began questioning what we were always told.

If more churches would welcome the honest questions of doubters and engage with the intellectual side of their faith, they would become safe places for those who experience doubt. If people don't feel understood, they are likely to find sympathy from those in the progressive camp who thrive on reveling in doubt. In progressive Christianity, doubt has become a badge of honor to bask in, rather than an obstacle to face and overcome.

The Moral Demands of Historic Christianity

In the early 2000s, ZOEgirl went on several mission trips with *Brio* magazine, an offshoot of the ministry of Focus on the Family. One of the young people I had gotten to know on two of these trips, whom I will call Sarah, was now an adult and in the process of coming out to all of her Christian friends. Deep down, I already knew what she was going to say when she called to tell me she was gay.

On one of the trips, she had confessed to me and a few other trusted leaders that she struggled with homosexuality. She had tried for years to change her feelings . . . to overcome the desires she didn't want and didn't choose. But in the end, she decided that God had made her this way and that it was his will for her to accept this as her identity. I told her I loved her and thanked her for telling me. Just before we hung up, I asked, "Sarah, can I ask you a question?"

"Sure," she responded.

"Would you say that you truly believe this is God's will for your life . . . or are you just tired of fighting?"

There was a long pause. In almost a whisper, Sarah responded, "I'm . . . I'm tired of fighting."

I can't imagine what it must have been like for Sarah to

grow up right smack in the middle of the American evangelical subculture of the early 2000s. A slightly awkward and boyish girl, she was down to earth, funny, and strong. She always had a smile on her face and possessed one of those magnetic personalities that seemed to draw everyone in. From the athletes to the girly-girls to the wallflowers—everyone liked her. And yet she carried this deep secret for so long.

My heart breaks when I think about it. Maybe she'd been offered a gospel that promised her health and happiness. Maybe she'd been spoon-fed too many sermons on self-esteem and following her dreams. Maybe her youth group spent too much time on games and pizza parties. Maybe her church had insinuated that anyone who experiences same-sex attraction is disqualified from Christian life. Whatever the reason, Sarah decided the cost of the true gospel was too high. The moral demands of biblical Christianity became too much for her, and she gave up.

I think of other friends who have same-sex attraction. Friends I love and care deeply about. I never think of this as only an issue . . . it has faces and names and stories and pain. And because I love them, I want to think clearly and truthfully about this issue. It's very clear that, from Genesis to Revelation, sex is extremely important to God. He created it and put important and life-giving boundaries on it for all of us. From cover to cover, the Bible teaches that sex is to be between a man and a woman in a marriage covenant for life. Any sexual act outside of that covenant is biblically defined as a sin. We cannot redefine what God calls sin and still presume to identify that ethic as Christian.

Sam Allberry, a pastor from the United Kingdom, shares in Sarah's struggle. From as far back as he can remember, he's been exclusively attracted to men. He has chosen to lay those desires aside for the sake of the gospel and has remained celibate all his adult life. In his book *Is God Anti-Gay?* he references a famous saying of Jesus in Mark 8:34: "Then he called the crowd to him along with his disciples and said: 'Whoever wants to be my disciple must deny themselves and take up their cross and follow me'" (NIV).

Allberry notes,

> It is the same for us all—"whoever." I am to deny myself, take up my cross and follow him. Denying yourself does not mean tweaking your behavior here and there. It is saying *"no"* to your deepest sense of who you are, for the sake of Christ. . . .
>
> Ever since I have been open about my own experiences of homosexuality, a number of Christians have said something like this: *"The gospel must be harder for you than it is for me,"* as though I have more to give up than they do. But the fact is that the gospel demands *everything of all of us.* If someone thinks the gospel has somehow slotted into their life quite easily, without causing any major adjustments to their lifestyle or aspirations, it is likely that they have not really started following Jesus at all.[4]

Jesus requires *everything of everyone.* But for some, it's not that they necessarily disagree with the core tenets of Christianity but that the cost of following them is just simply too high.

Even many Christians who don't experience same-sex attraction have adjusted their theology on the issue because they think it is the most loving stand to take. So in order to maintain some semblance of faith, they redefine Christianity and progress beyond its historic understanding, while others abandon the faith altogether.

Trouble with the Bible

Still others have trouble with the Bible itself. "Once upon a time, there lived a girl with a magic book" begins Rachel Held Evans's book on the Bible, *Inspired: Slaying Giants, Walking on Water, and Loving the Bible Again.*[5] As one of the most influential and prominent voices in the progressive Christian movement, Evans captivated thousands of readers with her insightful observations, witty prose, and engaging narratives. When she died unexpectedly in spring 2019 after experiencing an allergic reaction to a flu medication, both the evangelical and progressive worlds reacted with shock. Her death was even covered by many secular new outlets.

When I heard the news of her death, my eyes filled with tears. Having read her books, followed her blog, and even interacted with her on Twitter once, I felt a bit like I knew her. Her death was a shock and especially grievous considering she left behind a husband and two small children under the age of four. If it were me, I'd want people to pray for my kids, so that's what I did for her. I'd also want people to continue to take my ideas seriously, so that's what I will attempt to do whenever I interact with her writings in this book.

Evans was incredibly popular and persuasive because she had a knack for putting her finger on the pulse of common experience. She described her love for the Bible as a young girl who heard the echo of God's voice in every word. But then she recounted the disillusionment she suffered as she grew older and began to see the champions of her beloved Bible stories more like crooks and reprobates. When she read of the Israelites' conquest of Canaan, Noah's flood, and the death of every firstborn in Egypt, the God whose voice once echoed through her Bible's pages now seemed like a murderous scoundrel. She wrote, "If God was supposed to be the hero of the story, then why did God behave like a villain?"[6]

This reminds me of a woman I sat in class with week after week. She was a very thoughtful, compassionate, and all-around lovely person. A couple of weeks after my husband and I left the progressive church, she and I met for lunch at a local café. She understood why I'd decided to stop attending class and why I found the subject matter so disrupting to my spiritual walk.

But when I asked how she was doing, her eyes filled with tears as she expressed utter anguish over some of the more violent passages in the Old Testament. "I just can't believe God would kill all those children. I just can't," she disclosed with a quivering voice. She was talking about the verses in which God commanded the Israelites to wipe out the Canaanites in Jericho . . . every man, woman, and child. Her torment over this passage was tangible.

I didn't have an answer for her then, but when I later studied this account in the Old Testament, I learned that there was more going on in that situation than is often presented by skeptics and progressive Christians. For example, the Canaanites were so evil—so remarkably vile in their rebellion against God and all that is good—that if they were alive today, most of us would be crying out for justice, seeking to put a stop to their actions by whatever means necessary.[7] Plus, the progressive pastor hadn't presented all the information. It's likely that Jericho was more of a military outpost consisting of mostly male soldiers than a type of village where women and children lived.[8] I'm certainly not saying this makes it easy to swallow or solves all the tension, but to essentially present it as "Hey, God got mad and killed a bunch of kids" is a far cry from what actually happened. Honestly, the story *should* bother us. It shows us how God feels about sin and reveals how beautiful his plan of salvation is. But these ideas were typically not discussed in class. The Bible was presented as morally dubious in parts, and the only option offered was to reject or reinterpret the sections that didn't resonate.

Reconciling the character of God with his behavior is an issue that leads some Christians to question the reliability of what is written. As a result, many adopt a radically different way of reading and interpreting the Bible. We'll talk more about this in chapter 9.

The World Offers a More Attractive Option

Through the ages, Christians have encountered unbiblical worldviews and philosophies that have competed for their obedience and loyalty. These ideologies produce the values, beliefs, and moral codes that shape culture, and their adherents almost always present them as being morally superior to Christianity. To disobey or deny these tenets can make us social outcasts.

One such philosophy wielding significant influence in our current zeitgeist is critical theory.[9] Its formal beginnings are tied to the Frankfurt School in Germany in the 1920s and 1930s, and it was primarily a Marxist reaction against traditional theory, which sought to understand and describe the world from a neutral and objective perspective. Today, contemporary critical theory is understood much more broadly and is encapsulated in the large, multifaceted discipline of critical social theory. Critical theory understands and critiques power and oppression along the lines of race, ethnicity, class, gender, ability, sexuality, and many other factors.[10] This ideology sees the world as a struggle between oppressed groups and their oppressors. It then attempts to recalibrate power in favor of the marginalized and disenfranchised through emancipation, including formal academic efforts and grassroots activism.[11]

Another fundamental aspect of critical theory is its approach to gaining knowledge and apprehending truth. Through intersectionality, it prioritizes "lived experience" and identity rather than rationality in discovering and determining what is true.[12] In this paradigm, people's lack of privilege and their oppressed status give them greater discernment and a more complete view of the world. On the other hand, those with privilege and "oppressor" status are believed to have blind spots when it comes to understanding the world and discerning truth.[13]

As a result, critical theory adherents who see themselves as privileged recommend that we look to the marginalized for truth. Author and speaker Jen Hatmaker wrote that "when white, mostly male, straight married, able-bodied people with a certain threshold of money and power are at the center of the narrative, we will never correctly identify good fruit. . . . Privilege is a reliable enemy of discernment."[14] Interestingly, Hatmaker is white, straight married, and able-bodied, and she has a certain threshold of money and power. So according to her logic, the "privilege" she enjoys should make her mistrust her own views. Why then is she so confident in her own assertions?

Perhaps progressive author Sarah Bessey recognized this contradiction when she penned a blog post chronicling her journey toward becoming LGBTQ+ affirming. She wrote this disclaimer: "I—a white straight 18-years-and-counting married woman—am not the best *guide* for you. I can be *alongside* of you only. . . . After you read this, I encourage you to turn towards the margins and to let them lead you further out into God's shalom."[15] Bessey is using reasoning consistent with contemporary critical theory to explain that because of her class, gender, and ethnic background, she is not qualified to speak definitively on the issue of same-sex marriage. She encourages the reader to find truth by listening to those in the "margins."

Many Christians recognize the brokenness of our world—racism, poverty, and exploitation—and rightly want to do something about it. Contemporary critical theory can be an attractive way of looking at the world because it may seem like a loving and others-centered approach. Don't we want to free the downtrodden? Isn't that what Jesus came to do? But the problem with critical theory is that it isn't just a set of ideas that influences how someone thinks about oppression. It functions as a worldview, a way of seeing the world that answers questions like *Who are we? Why are we here? What is wrong with the world? How can this problem be fixed? What is the meaning of life?* When people adopt the tenets of critical theory, their answers to these questions are filtered through that lens. It's no wonder, then, that critical theory stands in contradiction to Christianity at many points.

Who are we? According to historic Christianity, we are human beings made in the image of a holy, loving, and just God. According to critical theory, our identity is not found in who we are created to be, but in how we relate with other groups as defined by our class, gender, sexual preference, and so on. *What is wrong with the world?* According to historic Christianity, sin against a holy God is what's wrong with the world. According to critical theory, oppression is what's wrong. *How can this be problem fixed?* According to historic Christianity, the sin problem is fixed by Jesus taking the punishment for our sins upon himself, dying the death we deserve, so we could be reconciled to God. But according to critical theory, the problem of oppression is fixed by activism, raised awareness, and the overthrow of oppressive systems and their power. *What is the meaning of life?* According to historic Christianity, it's to glorify God. According to critical theory, it's to free groups from oppression.

As Christians, we are called to do good works. In fact, James 2:26 tells us that "faith apart from works is dead." So naturally, a Christian will begin to produce these good works in response to their salvation. But when someone accepts the ideas of critical theory, it can begin to erode their Christian worldview by taking their eyes off the fundamental truths of who God is and how he works in the world. It excuses a person from upholding biblical morality and even considers the historic Christian sexual ethic to be oppressive. It can lead someone into progressive Christianity, which already devalues the historic Christian answers to these "worldview questions" and focuses on actions over belief. That becomes just another works-based gospel that ebbs and flows with cultural norms.

Hyperfundamentalism

The word *fundamentalism* is a loaded one. It can refer to an organized movement around the turn of the twentieth century that reacted against modernist theology. If you look up the word online, you will find various definitions—one of which is "a form of a religion, especially Islam or Protestant Christianity, that upholds belief in the strict, literal interpretation of scripture."[16] Fair enough. What does it mean to take the Bible literally? I've heard it said that it means to read the Bible *literally*. I agree. It means reading the Bible in the plain sense in which it's written. The Bible is a collection of books with different genres. There are poetry and metaphor and figures of speech. And unless you read "Under his wings you will find refuge" in Psalm 91:4 and believe this means God has feathers, you agree too.

Other definitions of fundamentalism are similar to this one from Dictionary.com: "Strict adherence to any set of basic ideas and principles." In this sense, everyone is a fundamentalist. Everyone has a set of principles they live by. In the progressive church, those principles might include tolerance (except toward conservative Christians) and inclusion (except for those who disagree with their interpretation of the Bible regarding sexuality). Ironically, this type of tolerance becomes its own legalistic fundamentalism.

Although the word *fundamentalism* has taken on a negative connotation (the last thing anyone wants to hear is "What are you . . . some kind of fundamentalist?!"), I don't mind saying I am a fundamentalist. Because you are too. We all are. What I have a problem with is what I would describe as hyperfundamentalism. This type of fundamentalism goes beyond the essentials of the faith. It is known by another name as well: *legalism*.

Many progressive Christians I meet grew up in impossibly strict sects of the faith that believed anyone outside their particular group was at best a nominal Christian and at worst a heretic. Because their faith communities had failed to teach them the difference between essential and nonessential beliefs, their entire foundation was rocked the first time they met a Christian who believed differently about the Rapture or the age of the earth.

One fellow class member recounted growing up in an incredibly legalistic, "my way or the highway" type of sect. This group considered themselves to be the only true church and believed that members of all other Christian denominations were on their way to hell. When he left home for the first time and met genuine believers who had never heard of his congregation (gasp!), it planted serious doubts about everything he'd ever been taught.

There is another expression of hyperfundamentalism—those heresy hunters who delight in pointing fingers. Driven by an insatiable appetite for controversy, they practically lick their chops waiting to identify the next false teacher. They run "discernment ministries" with websites attacking those who don't hold to their strict interpretations of Scripture regarding everything from whether the Spirit still gives the sign gifts to whether women should ever teach a group that includes men—for any reason—ever. I try to give as much grace as possible to Christians who disagree with me on issues that don't directly affect salvation. Perhaps growing up in environments where such grace was missing can cause confusion over what is essential versus nonessential.

The Problem of Suffering

It's the call you never think you're going to get. Sure, you've seen this scene play out in movies and maybe have even known someone who went through it. But this is the kind of thing that happens to *other* people. Not you. Not us.

Something they don't tell you in the movies is that upon

receiving cataclysmic news, your body betrays you. My knees began to shake wildly, and my throat became dry and my voice creaking.

After being rushed to the emergency room, my dear twenty-one-year-old nephew, Matthew, was gone. He had struggled with addiction for the past few years, and my sister lived in an almost constant state of worry. This night her darkest nightmare had become reality.

My mind spun, trying to make sense of the unthinkable. *But how can this be? He was so loved and cared for. I just played Ping-Pong with him two days ago at Thanksgiving. Just today I was writing about that stupid peach he threw when he was ten. How can this be happening?*

As an apologist, I talk and write about what we call "the problem of evil" all the time. It's one of the primary reasons many people lose faith in God and leave the church. Before Matthew's death, I connected on a certain level with questions like "How could a good God allow evil?" and "If God is all-powerful, why doesn't he stop bad things from happening?" But I had not yet faced them from the other side of harrowing grief.

Within the hour, I was looking at Matthew's body lying on a hospital bed with no life in his eyes. It was so quiet. No beeps or hums of machinery. No buzzing energy of doctors rushing in and out to check tubes, order tests, and record vital signs. When I looked at him, I felt a level of darkness I'd never felt before. It was as if all hope, light, love, joy, and goodness had been sucked out of the universe, and there was nothing but a doom-filled void. I didn't feel God's presence.

I didn't feel his peace. But I had walked in the excruciating darkness of doubt before, and I had learned to cry out to Jesus. I had learned to not walk by what I *feel* but by what I *know*.

"Jesus, please! Jesus, please! Jesus, please!" I shouted into that void over and over again. Slowly over the next few hours, little bits of light began to crack through that darkness to reveal—dare I say—the beauty of the wisdom of God. I don't understand this. I would do things differently. But I don't have all the information. My sovereign God does, and he knows the end from the beginning. He is trustworthy.

When I began writing this book, I had no idea that my own personal experience would become the story to illustrate this final point. My story has ended differently from some of the people who lost their faith because of abuse, doubt, or suffering. I cannot explain this, but I trust Jesus more today than I ever have. Through this ordeal, the gospel has never been more precious nor the Cross more beautiful to me. Because of the finished work of Jesus on that cross, death does not get the final word.

I don't have a pat answer to the problem of evil. But I know this: The promises of progressive Christianity offered me *nothing* through this trial. They offered my sister nothing. How could a weak view of God's Word, a disdain for the Cross, and a relativistic approach to truth bring my family any peace in this kind of adversity? In that hospital room, "my truth" was darkness. But "the truth" was true whether I felt it or not. God was there. God is sovereign. He is good and trustworthy. I've tasted and seen. My heart is resolute, echoing the sentiments of Peter, who answered Jesus after many had walked away from him, "To whom shall we go? You have the words of eternal life" (John 6:68).

When we are faced with immeasurable and unspeakable pain, we have a choice. We can open our hands to the Father and fall at his feet, or we can shake our fist at him and walk away. We can throw the raw magnitude of our doubts, questions, and piercing grief into his capable lap, or we can gather it all up into clenched hands and declare him incompetent . . . or nonexistent. We each have that choice.

My sister is a beautiful example of someone who placed every last shred of hope in Jesus. As she buried her youngest child—her only son—I was in awe of her faith. Did she have doubts and questions? Absolutely. We all did. But I stood in wonder as she clung to 1 Peter 4:12-13: "Beloved, do not be surprised at the fiery trial when it comes upon you to test you, as though something strange were happening to you. But rejoice insofar as you share Christ's sufferings, that you may also rejoice and be glad when his glory is revealed." Only within the framework of the historic Christian gospel do these statements bring any meaningful comfort. Only with a robust understanding of God's holiness, goodness, and sovereignty do these words give any hope.

Evil and suffering are ugly realities unleashed upon creation by sin, but our Savior stepped into our world, took on human flesh, suffered, and experienced death for us. When I saw Matthew's body lying on that hospital bed, I thought of Jesus. Jesus did that for me. For Matthew. For all of us. Jesus was well acquainted with grief and stood in our place.

He felt our pain and died the death we deserve. But the story doesn't end there. Jesus physically rose and defeated the power of sin and death forever. He didn't just come to feel our pain—he came to end it. He didn't just give us an answer to suffering—he became the answer. I long for the day when Revelation 21:4 will come to pass: "He will wipe away every tear from their eyes, and death shall be no more."

Matthew professed Christ and dedicated his life to Jesus a year before he died. He had been studying the Bible and had even begun writing Christian songs and talking with others about his faith. We are confident we will see him again, and that gives us great hope.

I cannot imagine walking through this ordeal without Jesus and the firm foundation of God's Word. I cannot imagine having any hope outside of the true gospel.

Growing Up in a Christian Bubble

While abuse, doubt, questions about Scripture and culture, hyperfundamentalism, and great suffering don't plague everyone, we have all been affected by the ease of amassing information and reading viewpoints contrary to our own. When I was a kid, there was no internet. There were no cell phones or social media sites. If you were super fancy, you might have had a "car phone," which was the size of a shoebox and cost about nine million dollars per minute to use. If you wanted to record your favorite television program, you had to set the timer on your VCR. If you missed it, or if the show was interrupted by "breaking news," you had to wait until the rerun aired later in the season. Otherwise you were out of luck—unless you lived in my house, where I am convinced my dad invented the first version of a DVR. He would set timers on multiple VCRs hooked up to two or three TVs. He then covered the front of the VCRs with duct tape to keep us kids from pressing the buttons and changing the settings—and if you touched that duct tape, you. were. dead.

That's just the way it was. Information wasn't as easy for us to access back then. For the most part, everyone watched the same nightly news, and our experience of Christianity was pretty much confined to what we heard within our local congregations or denominations. The Baptists thought the charismatics were crazy, the charismatics thought the Baptists were stuffy, the Presbyterians and Episcopalians just kept doing their thing, and we were all just fine, thank you very much.

And then the internet literally changed the world. All of a sudden, loads of information flooded our homes through that little glowing screen known as the personal computer. Skeptical claims and secular theories—which, in generations past, Christians lived entire lifetimes without hearing—were abruptly challenging our comfortable beliefs and confronting our deeply ingrained spiritual, sociological, and intellectual paradigms. We weren't in Kansas anymore, Toto.

This internet boom also brought scholarly arguments and debates about the Bible—which were once entertained among a much smaller circle of academics and professional intellectuals—into the mainstream. For many believers, especially those who experienced abuse or hypocrisy in church, or those who struggled with the Bible or the morality it teaches, or those whom the church brushed off as trouble-makers or pesky questioners, some of the more secular ideas became very attractive alternatives. On the other hand, the internet gave someone like me access to vigorous Christian scholarship that actually helped bolster and strengthen my faith.

The movement of progressive Christianity began with a legitimate desire for reform. But in seeking reform, its adher-ents found a false gospel. Although they aren't united around an official creed, progressive Christians are definitely united around a common set of (sometimes unspoken) *beliefs*. Like historic Christians, their beliefs are built around their responses to questions like "Why did Jesus die?," "What is the Bible?," and "What is the gospel?" While progressive Christians may bristle at concepts like certainty and the idea of landing concretely on answers, as we'll see in the next chapter, progressive Christians are quite dogmatic about *their* answers to these questions.

5

A Different Kind of Christianity

*Progressive Christianity is about not apologizing for
what we become as we live this life and openly engage
the faith we grew-up with. There are no sacred cows,
only the relentless, sacred search for Truth. Tradition,
dogma, and doctrine are all fair game, because all pass
through the hands of flawed humanity, and as such are
all equally vulnerable to the prejudices, fears, and biases
of those it touched.*

John Pavlovitz

The Emergent movement first became influential in the
evangelical church in the early 2000s. The Emergent Village
was founded in 1999 under the leadership of board members
that included Brian McLaren, Tony Jones, Diana Butler Bass,
Doug Pagitt, and other outside-the-box (and eventually identified as progressive) thinkers. Today, the Emergent Village
website is an online home and lifestyle magazine complete
with articles about gardening, decluttering your bathroom,
and achieving optimal bedroom lighting. But in the early
2000s, it was the hub of emergent Christians.

Born out of a belief that the church was much too influenced by modernism (the idea that truth could be found
through common sense, logic, human reason, and science),

the emergent movement sought to adapt Christianity to the postmodern mood that now dominated culture. In a nutshell, postmodernism rejects the idea that absolute truth can be known. With an emphasis on social activism and reaching those who were marginalized, oppressed, and forgotten by the hierarchical structures of the modern church, emergent Christianity was the new kid on the block that everyone wanted to know more about.

As someone who grew up doing homeless ministry and what might now be called social justice work, I was excited to see an awakening in the church on these issues in the early 2000s. Christians everywhere seemed to be curious about these new "missional" communities that were reexamining some of our long-held methods of doing church and living as Christians. Everything from the shallowness of cheesy church services to the problems we discussed in the last chapter, such as legalism and hypocrisy, was being looked at from a new perspective.

Mixing elements from many different denominational traditions (remember McLaren's seven Jesuses?), the emergent movement embraced ancient mysticism and focused on spirituality over religion. "Interfaith dialogues" became a regular practice among people who met to share stories and learn from other belief systems. Sometimes lines were blurred, and this caused Christian apologists and theologians to express concern over the general ambiguity surrounding the beliefs of those in the movement. In 2006, Emergent Village leader Tony Jones published an article written by theologian LeRon Shults explaining why their movement had no official statement of faith:

> Emergent aims to facilitate a conversation among persons committed to living out faithfully the call to participate in the reconciling mission of the biblical God. . . . A "statement of faith" tends to stop conversation. . . . Too often they create an environment in which real conversation is avoided out of fear that critical reflection on one or more of the sacred propositions will lead to excommunication from the community.[1]

Historically, Christians have viewed good works and acts of justice to be a *fruit* of their convictions. Believing the right things about God produces right actions. However, the emergent church flipped this on its head. Things like community, friendship, justice, and unity became the foundation upon which one's faith is built. In other words, what *someone does* became more important than what *someone believes*. (Even though you have to *believe* that statement is true to affirm it.)

Take the quote above. The logical problem with this idea is that the words themselves are statements—or more precisely, doctrines that one must believe in order to be accepted into their paradigm. What if I disagree about what it means to be a person "living out faithfully the call to participate in the reconciling mission of the biblical God"? As we've already discovered, many progressives strongly disagree with historic Christians on the reconciling work of Jesus on the cross. So what if I don't affirm the quote? Am I excluded from the community? I can tell you from experience that I am. Belief statements are unavoidable. These "nonstatements" end up being just as dogmatic as any faith statement progressives might be unintentionally criticizing.

Along with reexamining the methods of the church, some influential emergent thinkers began to reexamine the beliefs and doctrines of historic Christianity. No longer were they questioning only methods, traditions, practices, and philosophical approaches; they were also casting doubt on essential Christian doctrines themselves.

Because the term *emergent* is used much less frequently than it once was, many Christians think this movement is dead—that it was just a blip on the radar of Christian history. But Brian McLaren argues that it was simply forced underground. In 2012 he wrote,

> I think the movement is stronger than ever.
>
> In Evangelical and Charismatic circles, many Evangelical/Charismatic gatekeepers have successfully driven the emergent conversation underground....
>
> My sense is that more and more of us who are deeply involved with emergence Christianity are simply talking about God, Jesus, the Bible, mission, faith, spirituality, and life ... and doing so from a new and fresh perspective, but not using the "e" word so much. Sometimes it's the word "missional" that works, sometimes it's "progressive," sometimes it's "new kind of"—it goes under lots of labels.[2]

Anyone with a careful eye on the history and progression of the emergent movement can see that it is not dead. It is no longer underground. It is no longer a grassroots movement on the fringes of Christian culture. It has come out from the margins, stronger than ever but with a new name: progressive Christianity. The beliefs may be similar to those of the more liberal mainline denominations that burned through the church in the early 1900s. But progressive Christianity is a movement not satisfied to sit in the margins. It is directly aimed at infiltrating the evangelical church from within. This movement gives old theology a fresh face and a new name, and it is hell-bent on reforming the church according to its postmodern dogma.

What Do Progressive Christians Believe?

When progressive Christianity first hit the mainstream of evangelicalism in the late 2000s, I practically missed it. I had a new baby at home, ZOEgirl was no longer recording and touring, and all the intellectual energy I could muster was spent researching when and what to feed (and not feed) a baby. The internet chat rooms and forums I was spending most of my time in were those in which a bunch of moms discussed things like the best way to swaddle a newborn and which pacifiers could poison them with BPAs. I didn't realize that at the same time, the internet was abuzz with blogs, chat rooms, and message boards of lifelong Christians reexamining their beliefs and expressing their disillusionment and disappointment with the Christianity they had always known. I was late to that party, but the class with the progressive pastor was catching me up at top speed.

At first, progressive Christianity was a hodgepodge of beliefs. The leading voices in the movement were in various stages of deconstruction and reconstruction. Some still believed in the physical resurrection of Christ but were questioning the atonement. Others were still orthodox in their view of the atonement but were changing their minds on issues like homosexuality and abortion. Still others were more radical in their denials of certain essential doctrines, hoping to completely reframe Christianity for the postmodern world. But what united them all was a willingness to question the things historic Christians had believed and put their hope in for two thousand years.

Progressive Christianity has evolved since the early 2000s. There are concrete tenets I've discovered by reading and listening to the books, blogs, and podcasts of its leaders. Today there is general unity surrounding three topics: the Bible, the Cross, and the gospel.

The progressive views on everything from sexuality to politics to Christian life and practice are built on this foundation. As I've learned, progressive Christianity is not simply a shift in the Christian view of social issues. It's not simply permission to embrace messiness and authenticity in Christian life. It's not simply a response to doubt, legalism, abuse, or hypocrisy. It's an entirely different religion—with another Jesus—and another gospel.

As author Anne Kennedy writes,

We are not sitting at opposite sides of one long table. We are not eating of the one bread and drinking out of the one cup. We are talking about two different faiths, two different kinds of love, two different lords.[3]

As I sat in class with the progressive pastor, I became increasingly uncomfortable as he seemed determined to undermine our confidence in all three of these distinctives of historic Christianity. The practical outworkings of these progressive Christian beliefs lead to some dangerous places.

The Bible

"Is there anyone in here who *still* believes that Adam and Eve were literal people?" the progressive pastor asked the class with what sounded to me like smug confidence. The implication I took away was that *surely* none of the "peculiar" and enlightened people he had invited to his deconstruction party would still believe in such fairy tales. No one raised their hand—including me. What felt like a kick in the gut bent my body forward as I stared blankly into the top of the plastic folding table in front of me. Shame. That's what embraced me in that moment.

I know it matters that Adam and Eve existed, but I can't explain why.

How did I not even know this was a question?

Are there really Christians who don't think Adam and Eve were real people?

My inner monologue whimpered as the pastor went on to articulate his acceptance of Darwinian evolution and his skepticism of the biblical account. In future weeks he would go on to question the existence of Moses and Abraham. Jonah and David. He would challenge the authorship of the Gospels and the validity of the Virgin Birth. He read D. L. Moody's resolution to a supposed "Bible contradiction" and laughingly questioned it, with the rest of the class giggling along as if it were the silliest thing they'd ever heard. He praised those who didn't know what they believed and gazed with perplexed wonderment at those who expressed any kind of certainty (aka me).

Although class discussions revolved around many different topics of faith, the Bible was almost always at the center of conversation. It became clear to me that for people to deconstruct their faith—to begin pulling the thread of deeply ingrained beliefs—they had to first figure out what to do with the Bible.

As my friends in class embraced their processes of deconstruction, my social media news feed became peppered with articles by emerging progressive Christian bloggers. I recall reading an article in which the writer had just read a fairly comprehensive survey of church history. She gleefully pointed out that from the first century until now, Christians have vehemently disagreed on how to interpret the Bible. This led her to conclude that there is no one "right way" to read Scripture and that we should not claim to have the correct interpretation on any given topic.

Blog posts like these and comments from my classmates pushed me into studying Christian history in greater depth within the coming months and years. I read surveys of Christian history and books on apologetics and theology. But there came a point in time when I didn't want to simply trust someone else's analysis anymore. I wanted to read the church fathers for myself.

I started with Irenaeus, a theologian and apologist who lived in the second century. I first learned of him after seeing the 2014 movie *Noah*. After noting that Noah looked amazing for being six hundred years old (good job, Russell Crowe), I watched as the movie devolved into some unbiblical and downright weird mythology that I couldn't quite put my finger on. Then I read an article by a theologian who identified some gnostic themes in the film. He chided fellow Christian leaders for not recognizing it for what it was and suggested that no one should receive a seminary degree until they've "read, digested, and understood Irenaeus of Lyon's *Against Heresies*."[4] I wasn't trying to earn a seminary degree, but I took his advice and started my reading of the church fathers there.

As I dug into their writings, I was delighted to discover something so ancient yet so familiar—a deep love of Scripture and an almost indignant defense of the gospel. Yes, we've had doctrinal disputes, debates over interpretations, and arguments about application and practice. But the one thing that can be traced back through history to the genesis of Christianity is that the Bible—every word—is the Word of God. Things went off the rails from time to time, but from the beginning, Christians have been in agreement that the Bible is cohesive, coherent, inspired by God, and authoritative for our lives. In fact, one of the main issues Martin Luther had with the Catholic church was its progression beyond believing that the Bible alone is the authority for Christian life and practice. (Thus, the Reformation.) Luther's view matched that of ancient Christians.

Clement was a first-century believer who became the leader of the church in Rome. Tertullian, one of our church fathers, wrote that Clement knew the apostles personally.[5] Clement believed that Christians should obey the Scriptures because they are the words of God: "Let us act according to that which is written (for the Holy Spirit saith, 'Let not the wise man glory in his wisdom'). . . . Look carefully into the Scriptures, which are the true utterances of the Holy Spirit."[6]

Justin Martyr, who lived early in the second century, is often credited with being one of the first Christian apologists, and he, too, believed the Bible was divinely inspired: "When you hear the utterances of the prophets spoken as it were personally, you must not suppose that they are spoken by the inspired men themselves but by the divine Word who moves them."[7]

Irenaeus himself wrote some important works refuting heretical views that were infiltrating the church toward the end of the second century. He was discipled by a believer named Polycarp, who'd been personally discipled by the apostles.[8] Irenaeus's main arguments came from the Bible, which he clearly loved and held to be the perfect Word of God. Notice how he was careful to communicate that his own words were inferior to and under the authority of the Bible.

> The Scriptures are indeed perfect, since they were spoken by the Word of God [Christ] and His Spirit; but we, inasmuch as we are inferior to, and later in existence than, the Word of God and His Spirit, are on that very account destitute of the knowledge of His mysteries.[9]

There are hundreds of quotes I could include in this section, and I strongly encourage you to read the church fathers for yourself. Most of the writings of the fathers are free online. See for yourself what the earliest Christians believed about Scripture. Trace it through church history.

One of the fathers I most deeply connected with was an African theologian, St. Augustine of Hippo. I stumbled upon his book *Confessions* and found in its pages a brother in Christ who humbly approached his God with passion and intensity. With the intimacy of a memoir, the sophistication of a philosophical dissertation, and the tenderness of a brokenhearted child crying out to his father, *Confessions* transcends the signification of genre. As I read, I sensed that Augustine had written what my own heart would say if it could only find the words. Augustine's deep commitment to the veracity of the Scriptures is evident throughout:

> This Mediator, having spoken what He judged
> sufficient first by the prophets, then by His own
> lips, and afterwards by the apostles, has besides
> produced the Scripture which is called canonical,
> which has paramount authority, and to which we
> yield assent in all matters of which we ought not
> to be ignorant, and yet cannot know of ourselves.
> . . . For it seems to me that most disastrous
> consequences must follow upon our believing that
> anything false is found in the sacred books.[10]

Compare that to these words from progressive Lutheran minister Nadia Bolz-Weber:

> The Bible's not clear about s***! The Bible is a library.
> Let's say you have this huge library in your house
> and ask, "What's the clear message my library has to
> say about 'gender'?" The poetry is going to say one
> thing, history says another, prose says something,
> science fiction says something else.[11]

It's not difficult to see the difference in tone, reverence, and general approach to the Scriptures. As we'll see in chapter 9, the progressive view of the Bible is to see it as primarily a human book. Most progressives see the Bible as an archaic travel journal that documents what ancient Jews and Christians believed about God. Not all of it is authoritative. Not all of it is inspired. None of it is inerrant. Sometimes, if you look really hard, you might find the word of God *in it*. But it's up to you to decide which parts work for you and which parts don't. This is a radical departure from the historic Christian view of the Bible. As we'll see in chapter 9, it is a profound dismissal of how Jesus viewed the Scriptures.

All throughout church history, Christians have encountered these types of skeptical claims against the Bible. I'll echo what Augustine of Hippo wrote to a man named Faustus who, much like some of today's progressive Christians, was attacking the veracity and authority of the four Gospels. After thoroughly answering every claim, Augustine quipped, "You ought to say plainly that you do not believe the gospel of Christ. For to believe what you please, and not to believe what you please, is to believe yourselves, and not the gospel."[12]

The Cross

"I just can't believe in a God who isn't even as forgiving and caring as me. I can't believe in a God who isn't even as moral as me. I can't believe in a God who could torture his own son to death as some kind of payment. I could never do that to my child, and I just can't believe in a God who could."

I was perplexed by the words coming out of the mouth of a fellow class member during one particularly spirited class about the nature of sin, the Cross, heaven, and hell. When I asked him how he makes sense of what Paul teaches in his epistles about atonement, he hinted that he didn't really think Paul knew what he was talking about.

"But Paul got his theological training in heaven," I countered. "He was caught up to the third heaven and received revelations."

"Yeah . . . says him!" my classmate retorted.

Several of my fellow students were beginning to rethink the Cross. They were questioning the whole "Jesus died to pay for my sins" concept because they believed it implicated the character of God. If the Father required a blood sacrifice to atone for sin, it made him like a capricious pagan deity. If he desired that this sacrifice be made by his only Son, it made him something even worse: a cosmic child abuser.

Historically, Christians have believed that Jesus died for our sins . . . in our place . . . as our substitute. As we'll see in chapter 11, this was a choice Jesus made as God in flesh to redeem mankind to himself. Once again I turned to the early church fathers to see what ancient Christians had to say about the Cross.

In the late first century, Clement wrote that "Jesus Christ our Lord gave His blood for us by the will of God; His flesh for our flesh, and His soul for our souls."[13]

The Epistle of Barnabas is an early Christian document that was most likely written around the end of the first or early second century. Scholars aren't sure who wrote it, but it reflects Christian thought at the time, and some church Fathers ascribed it to Paul's coworker Barnabas. Its author clearly believed that the blood of Jesus brought about the forgiveness of sins: "For to this end the Lord endured to deliver up His flesh to corruption, that we might be sanctified through the remission of sins, which is effected by His blood of sprinkling."[14]

Another anonymous writing comes to us from somewhere around the early second century:

He Himself took on Him the burden of our iniquities,
He gave His own Son as a ransom for us, the holy
One for transgressors, the blameless One for the
wicked, the righteous One for the unrighteous, the
incorruptible One for the corruptible, the immortal
One for them that are mortal.[15]

Athanasius, one of the greatest theologians and defenders of the faith, wrote these words, probably in the early fourth century:

Taking a body like our own, because all our
bodies were liable to the corruption of death, He
surrendered His body to death *instead of all*, and
offered it to the Father. . . . He is the Life of all, and
He it is that as a sheep yielded His body to death *as
a substitute*, for the salvation of all.[16]

But again, don't take my word for it. The idea that Jesus died to pay the penalty of our sins is all over Scripture and the writings of the church fathers. Read for yourself. For example, Augustine of Hippo wrote,

But as Christ endured death as man, and for man;
so also, Son of God as He was, ever living in His
own righteousness, but dying for our offences, He
submitted as man, and for man, to *bear the curse*
which accompanies death. And as He died in the
flesh which He took in *bearing our punishment*, so
also, while ever blessed in His own righteousness,

He was *cursed for our offences,* in the death which He suffered in *bearing our punishment.*[17]

Contrast Augustine's words with these statements from progressive Michael Gungor:

I would love to hear more artists who sing to God and fewer who include a Father murdering a son in that endeavor.[18]

I simply think blood sacrifice is a very limited and less than timely metaphor for what the cross can mean in our culture.[19]

. . . that God needed to be appeased with blood is not beautiful. It's horrific.[20]

The progressive view of the Cross is that Jesus was killed by an angry mob for speaking truth to power. God didn't need his sacrifice, but in some way submitted to it in order to set an example of forgiveness for us all to follow. God didn't require blood—humans did. As progressive author Brian Zahnd wrote, "God did not kill Jesus; human culture and civilization did. God did not demand the death of Jesus; we did."[21]

As with skeptical attacks against the Bible, Christians have been answering these claims for the whole of our history. In his debate with Faustus, Augustine wrote,

The believer in the true doctrine of the gospel will understand that Christ is not reproached by Moses

when he speaks of Him as cursed, not in His divine
majesty, but as hanging on the tree *as our substitute,
bearing our punishment.* . . . If, then, you deny that
Christ was cursed, you must deny that He died; and
then you have to meet, not Moses, but the apostles.[22]

The gospel

"Who believes we were born good, and who believes we were
born sinners?" the progressive pastor asked in class one day.

He had just read the lyrics to a popular Christian song in
which the singer communicated his gratefulness to God for
saving such a sinful person. The pastor said, "I wish I could
tell this singer that they shouldn't see themselves that way.
They are so much more beautiful than that." I could only
assume that he had already answered the question in his own
mind and wanted to know who agreed with him.

I had learned by this point that if he was asking a question, there were really only two acceptable answers. If you
said, "I don't know," or took whatever view challenged the
accepted opinion of most Christians, you would be regarded
as open-minded and intelligent. If, on the other hand, you
affirmed or defended the historic view, you were dismissed
as someone who was just living in fear or brushed off as
someone who wasn't willing to intellectually engage the hard
questions of faith.

"I believe we were all born sinners," I chimed in after
several others expressed a lack of certainty on the topic.

"Why?" the pastor asked. But I wasn't sure why. I knew it
said so somewhere in the Bible, but I couldn't recall the verses

off the top of my head. It's not like we all had our Bibles open and were searching the Scriptures for our answers. Some students had expressed that certain Bible verses didn't "resonate" with them, so a few Bibles sat on the tabletops like random peculiarities you'd find in a curio shop.

I couldn't answer the pastor's why, but I knew in my gut that he was wrong. What I couldn't articulate at the time was that he was questioning the doctrine of original sin. Historically, Christians have believed that when Adam and Eve sinned in the Garden, a sin nature was passed down to all their descendants.[23] Put simply, original sin explains what's wrong with the world, and it's an integral part of the gospel because if nothing is broken, nothing needs to be fixed. The gospel means "good news" *because* it is the cure for the disease of sin.

The Bible teaches that God is holy, which by definition means he can't have any unity with sin. Theologian Wayne Grudem writes, "God's holiness means that he is separated from sin and devoted to seeking his own honor."[24] This puts humanity in quite a pickle. If we are all sinners, and God is separated from sin, that means he's separated from us. "The wages of sin is death" Paul tells us in Romans 6:23, so we desperately need to be saved. The Christian gospel can be best explained in four movements: Creation, Fall, Redemption, and Restoration. The gospel is God's plan to save, or redeem and restore, mankind.

Years later, after I had audited a theology class at a seminary, I was able to better express why original sin is true and why it matters. And as I studied church history, I learned that before the New Testament was written, the early church was unified in its belief about the gospel and expressed this belief in creeds and in something called *regula fidei*, or the rule of faith. Dr. Michael Kruger writes that "the rule of faith . . . is basically a convenient summary of what 'orthodox' Christians in the second century (and later) regarded as the earliest apostolic teaching."[25]

It's important to note that the early Christians weren't making things up. They were simply summarizing the teaching of the apostles as a way to preserve that teaching and pass it on to other Christians. Early apologists such as Irenaeus used this rule as the measuring stick to identify and call out heresy.[26]

Ancient writers expressed the rule of faith in distinct ways, but they all essentially said the same thing. There were debates and disagreements around nonessential and peripheral issues, but these early Christians were united on beliefs that were considered to be the nonnegotiables. In other words, they were united about the gospel.

Tertullian was a prolific and influential African Christian writer in the late second and early third centuries. He wrote,

Now, with regard to this rule of faith—that we may from this point acknowledge what it is which we defend—it is, you must know, that which prescribes the belief that there is one only God, and that He is none other than the Creator of the world, who produced all things out of nothing through His own Word, first of all sent forth; that this Word is called His Son, and, under the name of God, was seen "in diverse manners" by the patriarchs, heard at all times in the prophets, at last brought down by the Spirit and Power of the Father into the Virgin Mary, was made flesh in her womb, and, being born of her, went forth as Jesus Christ; thenceforth He preached the new law and the new promise of the kingdom of heaven, worked miracles; having been crucified, He rose again the third day; [then] having ascended into the heavens, He sat at the right hand of the Father; sent instead of Himself the Power of the Holy Ghost to lead such as believe; will come with glory to take the saints to the enjoyment of everlasting life and of the heavenly promises, and to condemn the wicked to everlasting fire, after the resurrection of both these classes shall have happened, together with the restoration of their flesh. The rule, as it will be proved, was taught by Christ, and raises amongst ourselves no other questions than those which heresies introduce, and which make men heretics.[27]

A similar version of this rule of faith was expressed by many different early Christian sources like Dionysius of Corinth, Justin Martyr, Aristides, Ignatius, Clement of Rome, Hippolytus, Irenaeus, Clement of Alexandria, Tertullian, and Origen. It also spanned geographical regions such as North Africa, Gaul, Rome, Syria, Greece, and Asia Minor.[28]

After reading and studying all the different versions

of the rule of faith, Dr. Michael Kruger summarizes early essential Christian belief this way:

1. There is one God, the creator of heaven and earth.

2. This same God spoke through the prophets of the Old Testament regarding the coming Messiah.

3. Jesus is the Son of God, born from the seed of David, through the virgin Mary.

4. Jesus is the creator of all things, who came into the world, God in the flesh.

5. Jesus came to bring salvation and redemption for those who believe in him.

6. Jesus physically suffered and was crucified under Pontius Pilate, raised bodily from the dead, and exalted to the right hand of God the Father.

7. Jesus will return again to judge the world.[29]

Dr. Kruger also points out that the rule of faith was not focused on one particular doctrine. It was intended to encompass the overarching narrative of God's great acts in history. This is the gospel of the ancient church. Note how it follows the narrative arc of Creation, Fall, Redemption, and Restoration.

Compare the rule of faith with these words from Brian McLaren about the progressive version of the gospel:

> [Jesus] came to announce a new kingdom, a new way of life, a new way of peace that carried good news to all people of every religion. A new kingdom is much bigger than a new religion, and in fact it has room for many religious traditions within it. This good news wasn't simply about a new way to solve the religious problems of ontological fall and original sin (problems, remember once more, that arise centuries later and within a different narrative altogether). It wasn't simply information about how individual souls could leave earth, avoid hell, and ascend to heaven after death. No, it was about God's will being done on earth as in heaven for all people. It was about God's faithful solidarity with all humanity in our suffering, oppression, and evil. It was about God's compassion and call to be reconciled with God and with one another—before death, on earth.[30]

These two gospels couldn't be more different. The rule of faith expresses a Creator God who became flesh and invites us to follow him in loving God and our neighbor. A God who was crucified, buried, and physically resurrected to save mankind from sin and death. A God who will return again to judge every single person who has ever lived and determine their eternal destiny. By denying original sin and God's plan to redeem humans and reconcile them to himself, the progressive gospel gives us an impotent deity who can only stand in "solidarity" with humans in our suffering and evil but can't cure it. This is not the gospel of Jesus. This is not the gospel of the apostles or ancient Christianity. It is not the gospel that can be traced through history to bring life and hope to Christians everywhere in the world today.

But I really can't stress this strongly enough: None of this is new. In *Against Heresies*, Irenaeus addresses the gnostic heresy that was masquerading as Christianity and deceiving many in the church. I was astonished to discover that what Irenaeus wrote in AD 180 could easily apply to the doctrinal and faith challenges we are facing in our current culture. The heretics in his day were not vitriol-spewing atheists bent on destroying the Christian faith from the outside. These were self-professed Christians who were determined to change it from within. They twisted the Scriptures and misrepresented tradition. Irenaeus wrote,

> These men falsify the oracles of God, and prove themselves evil interpreters of the good word of revelation. They also overthrow the faith of many, by drawing them away, under a pretence of [superior] knowledge, from Him who founded and adorned the universe; as if, forsooth, they had something more excellent and sublime to reveal, than that God who created the heaven and the earth, and all things that are therein. By means of specious and plausible words, they cunningly allure the simple-minded to inquire into their system . . . and these simple ones

are unable, even in such a matter, to distinguish falsehood from truth.

Error, indeed, is never set forth in its naked deformity, lest, being thus exposed, it should at once be detected. But it is craftily decked out in an attractive dress, so as, by its outward form, to make it appear to the inexperienced (ridiculous as the expression may seem) more true than the truth itself.[31]

As the writer of Ecclesiastes puts it,

What has been is what will be,
and what has been done is what will be done,
and there is nothing new under the sun.

ECCLESIASTES 1:9

When I was in class, every skeptical claim, cynical question, and progressive teaching the pastor was spouting was brand spanking new to me. Bless my heart, I assumed *he* had thought it all up. I had no idea that most of what he was saying was rooted in unorthodox thinking and had been refuted a hundred times over since the invention of the pen.

Like wheat and tares, true ideas and false ideas have grown together throughout church history, and it's up to faithful Christians to be watchful and diligent to compare every idea with the Word of God and see if it lines up. As my misgivings about the class at church grew, I realized that my differences with the progressives were much more substantial than I had realized at first—and that Christians have been fighting these battles for two thousand years.

6

Nothing New under the Sun

It's time for a new quest, launched by new questions, a quest across denominations around the world, a quest for new ways to believe and new ways to live and serve faithfully in the way of Jesus, a quest for a new kind of Christian faith.

Brian McLaren, *A New Kind of Christianity*

Growing up in Southern California had its perks. There was the glorious weather, beautiful mountains and beaches . . . and the excitement of the film and television industry. It was not uncommon to drive by our local park and see film crews shooting the latest episode of whatever drama or sitcom was popular at the time. Once my parents were asked to park their cars in the same place every day for two weeks because a B horror film was being recorded across the street and the producers needed the background to remain unchanged.

My best friend lived in Porter Ranch, where the iconic Halloween and police chase scenes were filmed for Steven Spielberg's classic movie *E.T. the Extra-Terrestrial.* After we saw the film, we ventured out to the empty field across the street from her house to search for the Reese's Pieces that Elliot famously dropped as bait to catch the beloved E.T. We didn't find any candy, but we did find the skid marks left by police cars in the notorious chase scene (or at least we convinced ourselves that's what they were).

From time to time, my family visited Universal Studios to take the world-famous tour. Boarding a tram, we rode around and saw the Bates Motel, were "captured" by Star Wars storm troopers, and crossed a bridge to view the site of my favorite show, *Gilligan's Island*. I was always struck by how small and underwhelming it was. To my young eyes, it seemed as if a grown man could walk across its entire diameter in ten steps or so. But perhaps nothing was quite as underwhelming as the "sea" over which Charlton Heston's Moses extended his staff to part the Red Sea in *The Ten Commandments*. Located fewer than a hundred yards from Gilligan's Island, the tram looked as if it were going to drive right into the water. Just in time, the sea would part, and the tram would cross on dry tracks and go up onto a bridge. Just as we were leaving, Jaws would jump out of the water right next to the tram and scare the daylights out of us. All of this happened in an area that seemed no bigger than an Olympic-size swimming pool.

Wheat and Tares

Just as Gilligan, Jaws, and Moses were all crammed around the same small body of water, good ideas and bad ideas are often found intermingled in the same space. Even in our churches, truth and lies can be wedged in like sardines, leaving many Christians confused and discouraged. Jesus told a story about it:

> The kingdom of heaven may be compared to a man who sowed good seed in his field, but while his men were sleeping, his enemy came and sowed weeds among the wheat and went away. So when the plants came up and bore grain, then the weeds appeared also. And the servants of the master of the house came and said to him, "Master, did you not sow good seed in your field? How then does it have weeds?" He said to them, "An enemy has done this." So the servants said to him, "Then do you want us to go and gather them?" But he said, "No, lest in gathering the weeds you root up the wheat along with them. Let both grow together until the harvest, and at harvest time I will tell the reapers, 'Gather the weeds first and bind them in bundles to be burned, but gather the wheat into my barn.'"
>
> MATTHEW 13:24-30

Jesus unpacked this parable for his disciples by explaining that he is the sower. The field is the world, the wheat is the "people of the kingdom," and the tares are the "people of the evil one."[1] And that pesky "enemy" that sows all the evil people among the wheat? That's the devil. The harvest is the end of the age, and the reapers are the angels. In this story, Jesus is predicting what it will be like for us as his church. He's basically saying that while we're here on earth, it's going to be a mixed bag. True Christians and false Christians will live together in the same world, even gathering together in the same sanctuary—in the same worship service—singing the same songs and listening to the same sermons. And to all those sickle-happy Christians who want to go ahead and weed out the tares now, he says wait. It's not our job, and if we made it our business, we'd inevitably have some wheat casualties on our hands.

This parable would have been more easily understood by a person living in the first-century Roman Empire because sowing tares in someone else's field was actually a thing—a kind of "primitive bioterrorism," as New Testament scholar Craig Blomberg puts it.[2] There were even Roman laws in place that prohibited it.

The word translated as "tare" in this passage is not just a generic word for weeds. It describes a specific weed, darnel, which looks very similar to wheat as it matures, but its grains are dark . . . and poisonous. If an ancient farmer found darnel among his wheat crop, he wouldn't try to uproot it first because he would probably lose some wheat in the process. He would wait until the whole field was ripe, at which time he could harvest the wheat. Some of the darnel might be uprooted in the process, but that didn't matter because the whole field would be weeded after harvest anyway.

Notice that in Jesus' parable the order of events is reversed. The tares are pulled up first, then the wheat. But the one doing the harvesting is no ordinary ancient farmer. Jesus will send his angels to weed out with razor-sharp precision "everything that causes sin and all who do evil" (Matthew 13:41, NIV), allowing the righteous to "shine like the sun in the kingdom of their Father" (verse 43, NIV). In other words, if *we* tried to remove the tares, we'd make a mess of everything and hack the field to pieces. For now, we must realize that wheat and tares will grow together looking very much alike.

So what are we to make of this? Does this mean we should never criticize or disagree with anyone? Does it mean we shouldn't call out error and name false teachers? On the contrary, the Bible overflows with passages encouraging Christians to do just that . . . to practice discernment.[3] This is what Christians have been tasked with since the very beginning. Why? Because Jesus predicted that wolves would invade his church. He warned that all kinds of false teachers and deceitful charlatans would rise up from within and present their bogus teachings as legitimate: "Beware of false prophets, who come to you in sheep's clothing but inwardly are ravenous wolves. You will recognize them by their fruits" (Matthew 7:15-16).

These teachers would look like sheep, talk like sheep, walk like sheep, and act like sheep. But these sheepy-looking beasts wouldn't be looking to snack on grass and clover. These would be carnivorous hunters looking to sink their chops into a nice juicy sheep steak. While wheat and tares represent true believers and false ones, a predatory wolf is a whole different animal. This can be especially confusing for the flock when the wolf in question is dressed up like a shepherd—the one person with whom the sheep are conditioned to feel safe. In class, I felt as if the pastor was presenting himself as just another sheep, humbly seeking truth and pursuing God. In the beginning I believed him. I thought we were on the same page. And because he was my "shepherd" who had won my respect and trust, I let my guard down.

Much of the New Testament, including the entire book of Jude, is dedicated to helping Christians watch out for, recognize, and avoid these sheep-clothed wolves. In researching some of these passages, I discovered that the topic of false teachers and false teaching is addressed directly in twenty-two of twenty-seven New Testament books. Encouragement to keep the true faith and to practice discernment is mentioned in every single one. Here is just a small sampling of what other New Testament writers have to say about false teachers:

> The time is coming when people will not endure sound teaching, but having itching ears they will accumulate for themselves teachers to suit their own passions, and will turn away from listening to the truth and wander off into myths.
>
> 2 TIMOTHY 4:3-4

In reference to Paul's letters, Peter writes,

> Some of his comments are hard to understand, and those who are ignorant and unstable have twisted his letters to mean something quite different, just as they do with other parts of Scripture. And this will result in their destruction.
>
> 2 PETER 3:16, NLT

False prophets also arose among the people, just
as there will be false teachers among you, who will
secretly bring in destructive heresies, even denying
the Master who bought them, bringing upon
themselves swift destruction.

2 PETER 2:1

Certain people have crept in unnoticed who long
ago were designated for this condemnation,
ungodly people, who pervert the grace of our
God into sensuality and deny our only Master and
Lord, Jesus Christ. . . . These people also, relying on
their dreams, defile the flesh, reject authority, and
blaspheme the glorious ones.

JUDE 1:4, 8

Notice the language here. False teachers creep in *unnoticed*
and *secretly* bring in distorted ideas about God. They appeal
to our passions and desires and tell us what we want to hear.
They don't announce themselves wearing sandwich boards
that say, "Hi, I'm a false teacher. Let me scratch those itching
ears!" They look like us, talk like us, act like us, and claim
to be one of us. It's easy to see why they are so effective in
tricking many unsuspecting believers.

Class Notes

With each meeting, my discomfort over what we were
discussing in class grew more painful and pointed. I constantly scolded my inner monologue for being so judgy, but

simultaneously I was utterly convinced that the class was heading in the wrong direction.

One afternoon, I became distressed about what seemed like a profound disregard for the fear of God among my classmates, and I burst into tears just as the meeting was about to wrap up. The progressive pastor called me later and suggested I meet with a woman in the church who was a licensed therapist. This seemed to me like code for "Clearly this is *your* problem. You just need to get over whatever childhood trauma is causing you to react so emotionally to all of these brilliant new observations about Christianity and fall in line."

Within a week I found myself in her cozy, naturally lit office. When I began to describe the discomfort I had been experiencing with the books, teachings, and discussions being facilitated by the pastor, she grabbed two fun-size Mars bars from the candy bowl on her desk. She laid them side by side and asked me to imagine her opening one of them and putting a different wrapper around it. That piece would still be a Mars bar . . . just in another wrapper. She told me that was what the pastor was doing—giving me the same candy with a different label.

My inner monologue quipped, *She has it backwards.* "It seems to me that he's putting the same wrapper on two entirely different kinds of candy," I replied. "It looks the same on the outside, but the core of it is very different." Wheat among tares.

Errant teaching is nothing new; it emerged in the church almost from the beginning. Christianity hadn't even gotten its foot off the proverbial starting block before counterfeit gospels began to infiltrate and influence the early church. In other words, almost as soon as there were sheep, there were wolves.

One way to spot them? Each seemed to recast Jesus' command to his disciples that "whoever wants to be my disciple must deny themselves and take up their cross and follow me" (Matthew 16:24, NIV).

Same Wrapper, Different Candy #1: The Circumcision Party

> Then Jesus said to his disciples, "Whoever wants to be my disciple must circumcise themselves and follow me."
>
> 1 JUDAIZER 16:24

Although there is no book of 1 Judaizer, if it existed, a passage like the one above would certainly be at its center. Also called the Judaizers, the circumcision party was a group of Jews who taught that if Gentiles were going to become Christians, they had to first conform to Jewish customs. In other words, they had to become Jews before they could become Christians. Considering that the Jewish rite of passage was circumcision, it doesn't take much imagination to understand why this was particularly upsetting to the adult male Gentile population.

In his letter to Titus, Paul explained the character qualities and traits that church elders needed to possess. Along with being self-controlled, humble, disciplined, and holy, they needed to acquire the skill of refuting false doctrine. Why? Because of the Judaizers, or circumcision party—the first heretical group to spring up among Christians. Here's how Paul described them:

> There are many who are insubordinate, empty talkers and deceivers, especially those of the circumcision party. They must be silenced, since they are upsetting whole families by teaching for shameful gain what they ought not to teach.
>
> TITUS 1:10-11

The Judaizers were distorting the gospel, and Paul became so frustrated with this particular group of wolves that he suggested they go all the way and castrate themselves (Galatians 5:12). The circumcision party's influence was so widespread that big chunks of the New Testament (particularly in Galatians, Titus, Acts, and 1 Timothy) are dedicated to refuting their teaching and warning believers about them. According to Galatians 2:11-14, even Peter was intimidated by this prominent group!

The circumcision party was trying to *add* something to what Jesus accomplished. As I've heard my current pastor repeat on many occasions, the easiest way to spot heresy is to remember this: Jesus + *anything* = a false gospel. For the circumcision party, it was Jesus + circumcision.

The matter was settled at the first of many councils convened throughout church history to respond to different heresies. This council is recorded in Acts 15, in which Paul,

Barnabas, Peter, and James all chimed in with their arguments against this emerging blasphemy. The first heresy in church history was dealt with, and the council was a model for church leadership for years to come.

It can be easy for Christ followers to fall into the trap of adding something to the gospel, whether we look to a certain political party to rescue us or wonder if we'll earn favor with God by being "super Christians" who never miss morning devotions. However, with their denial of the atoning work of Jesus on the cross, many progressive Christians take it one step further: Jesus is no longer our Savior but an example of how we can do good works in the world and forgive others. That has become the highest virtue, and all other truth claims are judged by it. Thus the progressive gospel is Jesus + social justice.

Same Wrapper, Different Candy #2: The Gnostics

> Then Jesus said to his disciples, "Whoever wants to be my disciple must find the divine spark within herself and follow my hidden wisdom."
> GNOSTICUS 16:24

As I explored heresies in the early church, I was struck by how widespread and diverse the beliefs of a group which came to be known as the Gnostics were in the first centuries after Christ. In the fifth century, Augustine famously refuted the Manichaeans, a sect that shared some similarities with Gnosticism and that he himself had been a part of before his conversion to Christianity. The Manichaeans saw the world as a fight between the spiritual world of light and the material world of darkness. This, along with a focus on what we might articulate today as "finding yourself," was a common theme among Gnostics of all stripes. And while no book of Gnosticus exists, the Gnostics did articulate a gospel that was much different from what we find in Scripture.

The church father Irenaeus wrote the magnum opus on heresy around AD 180, addressing some gnostic ideas that were coming into the church. To modern readers, it's weird and fascinating. However, to ancient people steeped in the works of Greek philosophy, gnostic speculations didn't seem that uncommon. There's a spiritual universe called the Pleroma, which includes an evil Demiurge and his mother, Sophia. There's Monogenes, who gave birth to the "Father" and the "Holy Spirit." There are emanations and Aeons and a divine mother named Achamoth, or more commonly, Barbelo. With different expressions of Gnosticism among various groups of people, it can be difficult to nail down a common theme. At times it feels like you're reading an ancient religious writing, and at other times it feels like you're reading training materials for some bizarre modern cult. But all that strangeness aside, there is a practical element to Gnosticism that resonates with many modern assumptions.

The word *gnosis* simply means "knowledge." Gnosticism wasn't about sin. In fact, Gnostics didn't believe that the world was broken because of Adam's choice to sin against

God. They believed it was corrupted because of the evil demiurge who created it and rules over it. The only "sin" was ignorance. Gnostics, therefore, believed that Jesus came not to save us from sin but to impart special knowledge that would essentially lead us to participate in the divine pleroma. To find this knowledge was to find salvation. "The freedom of the gnostic is freedom from subjection to the heavenly ruler, the evil demiurge. This freedom is attained by him by participation in the divine realm, the pleroma."[4]

The early Gnostics tried hard to popularize their ideas among Christians by claiming to be Christians themselves and by using Scripture alongside their own texts to "prove" their ideas. Irenaeus explained that they not only used the writings of the New Testament to demonstrate their "perverse interpretations" and "deceitful expositions" but that they also interpreted parables and allegories from the Old Testament in a duplicitous and fraudulent manner.[5]

In the introduction to Irenaeus's *Against Heresies*, John Arendzen wrote,

> When Gnosticism came in touch with Christianity, which must have happened almost immediately on its appearance, Gnosticism threw herself with strange rapidity into Christian forms of thought, borrowed its nomenclature, acknowledged Jesus as Saviour of the world, simulated its sacraments, pretended to be an esoteric revelation of Christ and His Apostles, flooded the world with apocryphal Gospels, and Acts, and Apocalypses, to substantiate its claim.[6]

As odd as Gnosticism may sound to us now, it captured the minds of many Christians who were already acquainted with similar types of speculation found in the Greek thinking of the day. Like the progressive Christianity we find in our culture, it mimicked Christianity in many ways, using some of the same language and even acknowledging the Father, Jesus Christ, and the Holy Spirit. It imitated the sacraments.[7] It used Scripture to support its ideas. It believed it was the true expression of Christianity. Gnostics viewed themselves as much more "enlightened" than the simple folks who believed that Jesus died to atone for their sins. Instead, they saw him as making right a corrupted cosmos that the evil demiurge had created.

There are many striking similarities between old-fashioned Gnosticism and progressive Christianity. With its use of Christian language, sacraments, and Scripture, and its pursuit of self-acceptance, it thrives on viewing itself as a more enlightened and mature version of Christianity. John Zmirak made this point with more than a hint of stinging sarcasm in an article he wrote in 2017 entitled "Progressive Christians Are the Best Christians in History. Just Ask Them!" He wrote,

> Perhaps the reason that they reject what every previous generation of Christians believed on a long list of subjects is that these people have finally discovered what Jesus really meant by all that He said and did. Maybe that's the answer![8]

Brian McLaren argues for this type of thinking quite fervently in his book *A New Kind of Christianity*. As we'll see in chapter 9, McLaren believes that Christians today have a more mature view of God than our predecessors who wrote the Bible did. Pitting the earliest biblical writers against the more enlightened voices who came later, he traces the "gradual maturing" of these biblical writers from simplistic and downright wrong to more mature and correct. He even points out that some images of God in the Old Testament are "unChristlike."[9] For McLaren, this culminates in the "higher and wiser" view of God that we have today.[10]

Gnostic teaching claimed something similar in the era of the early church. According to Gnostics, the Creator God of the Old Testament was incorrectly identified in Scripture as the *only* God. Although the Gnostic myth has many variations, Gnostics teach that there were sources of special knowledge that emanated through Aeons from another supreme being beyond the Creator God of Old Testament literature.

Notice the similarities in thought patterns between the Gnostics and today's progressives. Both claim sources of knowledge outside the Bible that can and should judge Scripture. The problem with McLaren's position is that there is nothing but our own personal sense of right and wrong (which will most often be informed by our cultural assumptions) to judge what is "right and wrong" in the Bible.

This is something C. S. Lewis referred to as "chronological snobbery." He described it as "the uncritical acceptance of the intellectual climate common to our own age and the assumption that whatever has gone out of date is on that account discredited."[11] He encourages good thinkers to ask questions like "Why did this idea go out of date?" and

"Was it ever refuted or did it simply become unfashionable?" and "If so, who refuted it? How? Why?" It's about having the humility and intellectual honestly to admit that the time we now live in is also a period in the history of the world. We, like all the people who have gone before us, are influenced by our cultural paradigms, societal norms, and collective intellectual assumptions. Just because our culture has come to a consensus on something does not make it true or right. Remember . . . there was a time in history when the cultural influencers pretty much agreed that slavery was just fine. And many of them even twisted the Bible to justify that belief, which is why good hermeneutics is so important.

Like Gnosticism, progressive Christianity is built upon a foundation of the "new." As we'll see in chapter 9, this even applies to their view of the Bible. According to progressive Christians, we have been wrong about the Bible. Have we just now, two thousand years later, discovered the right way to read it? Has God finally revealed the correct way to interpret and apply the Scriptures to a select few of the most affluent people of Western civilization? I think not.

The progressive gospel is Jesus + new knowledge.

Same Wrapper, Different Candy #3: The Marcionites

> Then Jesus said to his disciples, "Whoever wants to be my disciple must reject ideas like hell and judgment, and simply follow my life of love and compassion."
> 2 MARCION 16:24

Around the middle of the second century, a teacher named Marcion began gaining followers and influencing the church. He saw the teachings of Jesus as wholly inconsistent with the mean-spirited, jealous, and wrathful God he perceived in the Old Testament. He believed that the God of the Old Testament and the God of the New Testament were two different deities, with the former being an inferior, wicked, and petty being and the latter being loving and all-forgiving. In stark contrast to the circumcision party, Marcion believed that the Old Testament law was violent and contradictory. Therefore, anyone who adhered to Old Testament beliefs and practices was going against Christianity.

Marcion based his theology on the recorded sayings of Jesus and some of the letters of Paul, whom he accepted as a true apostle because Paul taught that Christians were not obligated to follow Old Testament law. Marcion famously formed his own canon of Scripture, which of course excluded the entire Old Testament. In fact, it included only ten epistles of Paul along with a version of the Gospel of Luke he edited to reflect his belief that Christianity should be freed from its Jewish context.

Ultimately, the Marcionites rejected all aspects of God and Christianity that included wrath, hell, or judgment. Marcion was excommunicated in AD 144, but his ideas live on because—let's face it—it's much easier to remove the uncomfortable parts of the gospel and embrace the feel-good part. But as we'll discover in chapter 10, a God without wrath is a God who can't save you, and that is not good news for anyone.

With its view of the Old Testament God as petty and spiteful, its denial of God's wrath and hell, and its discomfort with the blood atonement of Jesus, progressive Christianity looks a bit like warmed-over Marcionism.

Much like Marcion, Brian McLaren believes that the God we find in the Old Testament is different from the "just, holy, and compassionate God and Father of our Lord Jesus Christ"[12] we find in the New Testament. He writes that in the Hebrew Scriptures, he finds "a character named 'God' who sends a flood that destroys all humanity except for Noah's family," does a good bit of "smiting," and directs former slaves to go to war with surrounding nations. In fact, he refers to these actions as "crimes."[13] But by viewing the Bible as a record of the gradual maturing of humanity's understanding of God, he is able to shrug off the more difficult passages describing God's judgment and acts of justice.

In this case, the heresy is Jesus *minus* something. The progressive gospel is Jesus minus judgment.

We need to be diligent about spotting elements from other heresies that reappear at various times throughout church history. There was Arianism, which denied the deity of Jesus; Pelagianism, which denied original sin; and Patripassianism, a belief that God the Father became incarnate and suffered on the cross.[14] After the Reformation there was Socinianism, which rejected original sin, the Trinity, and substitutionary atonement.

Like the unorthodox movements that came before them, progressive Christians are not teaching anything new. They are simply giving old ideas a new voice, a distinct spin, and an updated image. And the apostle Paul warned two millennia ago that this would happen:

> I am astonished that you are so quickly deserting him who called you in the grace of Christ and are turning to a different gospel—not that there is another one, but there are some who trouble you and want to distort the gospel of Christ. But even if we or an angel from heaven should preach to you a gospel contrary to the one we preached to you, let him be accursed.
>
> GALATIANS 1:6-8

As I researched the different heresies of the early church, I received tremendous comfort from the knowledge that God has not left us uninformed, unequipped, or ignorant. He has not left us unarmed against these attacks on his truth. He has given us something so incredible, so astoundingly beautiful, so precious that it compelled the nineteenth-century Scottish minister Robert Murray M'Cheyne to declare, "One gem from that ocean is worth all the pebbles of earthly streams."[15]

God gave us his very Word. He gave us the Bible.

If there was one thing I'd always had in common with the historic expression of Christianity, it was a deep love for Scripture, the place to which I had always turned to get to know God and learn about his plan for mankind. But now as I turned to my well-worn Bible with fresh eyes and new questions, I was bothered by the possibility that I might find a crack in the foundation. Was I about to discover something that would topple the whole thing?

7

For the Bible Tells Me So?

What good is it to say that the autographs (i.e., the
originals) were inspired? We don't have the originals!
We have only error-ridden copies, and the vast majority
of these are centuries removed from the originals and
different from them, evidently, in thousands of ways.

Bart Ehrman, *Misquoting Jesus*

I received my first real Bible when I was about nine years old.
It was a burgundy bonded-leather, large-print edition of *The
Living Bible* with my name embossed in gold at the bottom
right corner: *Alisa Girard*. My very own Bible. I treasured it.

"Where do I start?" I asked my mom. She suggested I
begin with Proverbs.

"Proverbs 3 was the first chapter I read in this Bible" is
handwritten on a page of notes in the back. Underneath that,
"GOOD VERSES" is written (in all capitals, of course), and
in this section, I wrote word for word all the "good verses" I
could find. One notable entry was Proverbs 22:15: "A young-
ster's heart is filled with rebellion, but punishment will drive
it out of him," to which I added "/her." I circled "her."

The first verse I highlighted in this cherished Bible was Proverbs 3:6: "In everything you do, put God first." This made more sense to me than anything I had ever read. It got into me. I just knew this book spoke truth. I knew it was straight from the mouth of God and I could live my life by it. My parents taught me this as well—it was the water I swam in.

I loved reading the Bible. As early as I learned to read and write, I read and studied what was written on its pages—and it was alive. I walked in the Garden with Adam and Eve, pondering whether I would have eaten the fruit. (I would have.) I wondered about the snake . . . could they all talk back then? Why was he cursed to slither on his belly? Did snakes originally have legs?

I boarded the ark with Noah and his family, and with chilling soberness sailed away from all the people left behind. Did they try to swim toward the ark, screaming and pleading to be let on board? Did their fingernails claw at the boat as they realized their mistake? (Side note: I was an intense kid. I wasn't one of those frilly-bow-and-tights-clad girls who colored pictures of Noah's ark on Sunday, assuming it was a happy story about a floating zoo.)

I felt the palpable fear and reverence of Moses when I stood with him before the burning bush. I rode into battle with Deborah when her army commander was too afraid to go alone. And Jael—the Kenite housewife who ended the Canaanite attack on Israel by using a mallet to drive a tent peg through the head of their leader—I really liked her. I saw myself in the story of David and Goliath as the young shepherd answered the rebellious giant's taunts of defiance with a declaration that the battle was the Lord's. (Of course, when I read the story in 1 Samuel 17, I was David. I wasn't among the panic-stricken Israelites waiting for someone to save them—who for forty whole days couldn't find even one guy to go and fight the Philistine champion. But age and wisdom have taught me that I am actually more like the terrified Israelites.)

I found myself in Esther's story, fasting and praying. Learning to trust God even if it meant risking my life to obey him and saying along with her, "If I perish, I perish." I sang through the Psalms and gleaned from the wisdom of Job, Proverbs, and Ecclesiastes. "Don't let the excitement of being young cause you to forget about your Creator. Honor him in your youth before the evil years come" was written on my heart. I read Song of Solomon with delight at the thought of my husband one day calling me, "O woman of rare beauty."[1] I giggled at breasts being compared to gazelles and heeded the wisdom of not awakening love before its time. (This kept me from even kissing a guy until my early twenties.)

I sympathized with Jeremiah, who thought he was too young and incompetent to serve God. I deeply resonated when he wrote that God's words were his joy and heart's delight. I commiserated when he was persecuted and reproached . . . sitting alone because of God's hand. He was putting God first, just like I'd read in Proverbs 3:6. I stood in the fiery furnace with Shadrach, Meshach, Abednego, and Jesus—with Russ Taff's eighties hit "Not Gonna Bow" playing like a soundtrack in the flames.

I marveled at Jesus, who could in one breath offer rest for all who would come to him, and in the next, address the religious leaders as a brood of vipers. A man who was laid in a smelly manger at birth yet claimed to sit on the throne of the universe. A man whose first uttered sounds were the cries of a newborn baby yet who appeared in Revelation with a sword in his mouth and a voice like rushing water. A man who split history in two and challenged every person who would ever live to either call him a liar or worship him as Lord. I sat amazed as he raised a twelve-year-old dead girl to life with the Aramaic words *"Talitha cumi"*—"Little girl, I say to you, arise" (Mark 5:41). Something deep inside me knew he was also talking to me. I had once been dead in my sin and in need of his resurrection. The Word of God was speaking to me. *Talitha cumi.*

I stood with Mary at the cross, watching Jesus' sweat and blood drip down its beams. I watched him struggle for breath as he finally cried out, "It is finished."[2] Somehow I knew that everything I had read in the Bible was pointing here. To this moment. To the Cross. Jesus was my ark. My giant-slaying Savior. My fourth man in the fire.

I read the Gospels, the Epistles, and the rest of the New Testament. I read the entire Bible (minus a few sections of Numbers) by the time I was twelve. I didn't understand it all, but I would grab little phrases here and there from my *Living Bible.*

"Continue to love each other." (Hebrews 13:1)

"Whatever is good and perfect comes to us from God." (James 1:17)

"Don't let anyone think little of you because you are young." (1 Timothy 4:12)

"See, I am coming soon." (Revelation 22:12)

Class Notes

Before starting the class, I was absolutely and wholeheartedly convinced that the Bible was the Word of God—inspired, inerrant, and infallible. But other than having been taught that, *I had no idea why I believed it*. One day in class, the progressive pastor asked, "How many of you believe the Bible is God's Word?" I raised my hand, along with one other woman.

"Why?" he asked, short and simple.

The other woman answered, "Because I can feel it. It's something that resonates so deeply in my heart—it's palpable."

To this the pastor replied, "Does the Bible have final say?"

"Yes, final say," she answered with a businesslike confidence, tapping her open hand on the table in front of her. I was really glad she was in class that day. She was a guest . . . a friend of the pastor's and a fairly well-known women's speaker. I was thrilled not to be the only one disagreeing with him for once.

Looking thoughtfully at her, he replied, "I've met Muslims who say the exact same thing about the Quran. They say it's something they feel deep in their hearts. One Muslim friend even used the word *palpable* as well."

I looked at the other woman, hoping she would have an answer, but she seemed to be struck mute by his counterpoint. She just sat there quietly as a few awkward moments passed.

Right then and there, I realized that I had based my whole life on a book, and I had no intellectual reason to explain why. This was a turning point. In the past, I had never been swayed by arguments against Christianity because I *just knew* the Bible was true. If someone suggested that Jesus wasn't really raised from the dead or that humans evolved from apes, I would just consult my Bible and prove them wrong. "The Bible says . . ." was all I needed to end a line of questioning.

But now someone had knocked the legs out from under the Bible—and I had nothing. The truth is, I didn't know why I believed that the Bible that sat in my lap contained the same words that were written thousands of years ago. I didn't know how the Bible was compiled, canonized, copied, and translated. I didn't know why I believed that the Gospels were written by eyewitnesses of Jesus' life. I didn't know the difference between me and the Muslim who felt exactly the same way about his Quran as I did about my Bible. We were both convinced that we had found the real God. We were both persuaded in the depths of our souls that our holy book was the right one. We both *fully believed* we were right. *But we couldn't both be right* because the Bible and the Quran contradict each other on many points.

Take, for example, the issue of Jesus' death. Remember in chapter 1 where I mentioned that Christianity stands or falls based on the resurrection of Jesus being a real historical event? The Quran teaches that Jesus didn't die on the cross. If the Quran is right and Jesus didn't die, he couldn't have been resurrected, and Christianity would be proven false. But if the Bible is right and Jesus died on the cross and was resurrected, Islam would be proven false. These are high stakes. Due to these contradictions, there is no warm and fuzzy "my truth" when it comes to the historical facts. Jesus either died on the cross or he didn't. I *needed* to know why I believed the Bible got it right. And I needed to be willing to abandon that belief if it wasn't true.

I embarked on a journey to discover the reliability of the Bible, and I started with the New Testament. I needed to ask a couple of important questions that would help me nail down what really matters:

Do we have an accurate copy of what was originally written?

Do those records tell the truth about Jesus, his life, and his teachings?

If I could get to the bottom of those two questions, I would have a good place to start. I suspected there was a good reason so many Christian scholars, pastors, theologians, and laypeople had trusted the New Testament for two thousand years, but now I needed to find out why for myself.

Do We Have an Accurate Copy?

At first I read a few apologetics books that made convincing cases for the reliability of the Bible. But as a chronic overthinker and naturally skeptical researcher, I didn't just want to read an analysis of what the scholars were saying. I wanted to hear from the scholars themselves. Even better, I wanted to read the primary sources the scholars were reading and analyzing. On that journey, I discovered textual criticism, a branch of scholarship dedicated to studying the existing manuscripts of ancient texts. For a flaky artist like myself who's practically allergic to words like *scholarship* and *textual*, this sounded like a highly intellectual pursuit. I pictured snooty professors staring down their noses and laughing at the simpletons who didn't know the difference between prelapsarianism and postlapsarianism. (Google it.) But it also made me feel better to know that this was an actual science . . . with actual scholars . . . who had actual PhDs . . . from actual universities like Princeton and Cambridge. This wasn't just information invented by some wacko with a blog. This was a real thing.

I learned that textual criticism is a discipline that doesn't just apply to the Bible. It's the method scholars use to reconstruct the wording of any ancient writing for which we no longer have the original documents. So if you've ever read Plato's *Republic*, Homer's *Iliad*, Aristotle's *Rhetoric*, or Shakespeare's *Romeo and Juliet*, you can thank a textual critic.

How does it work?

I began to read anything on textual criticism I could get my hands on. I listened to debates, lectures, and online seminary courses. I learned from scholars who believe the Bible is reliable, and from those who don't. I read liberal, conservative, evangelical, progressive, and even atheist scholars.

I discovered that New Testament scholars disagree on *a lot* of things. (That's putting it mildly!) If I wanted to find a scholar to tell me the Bible is a mess of corrupted material that's full of contradictions, I could find one. If I wanted to find a scholar to tell me the Bible is God's very words written down perfectly and preserved without error, I could find one of those, too. So instead of picking the scholar who most agreed with what I *wanted* to be true, I decided to figure out which facts they all generally agree upon. (For the record, this is a really good starting point if you feel confused about all the mixed messages coming from authorities in any field of study.)

Can I step on a soapbox for a second? Of course, there are always the extreme "fringe" scholars on both sides of any issue. For example, most New Testament scholars, Christian and atheist, agree that Jesus existed as a historical person—but that doesn't mean you can't find a scholar here and there to claim otherwise. And make no mistake . . . *all scholars* have biases. Let's say that again together: *All scholars have biases.* Don't let a skeptic convince you to throw out scholarship that has been carefully researched and reasoned by confessing Christians because of their "pro-Christian bias." Atheist scholars have biases too. For example, most atheist scholars will tell you that supernatural events in the Bible like miracles didn't really happen. This isn't because they have evidence to support their conclusion . . . they simply *assume* biblical miracles didn't happen because they also have a bias: It's called an antisupernatural bias. So in my opinion, the most reliable scholars are the ones who admit their bias, are honest about it, and try their best to be impartial. The ones who don't recognize their bias? Those are the ones who will be most influenced by their unacknowledged presumptions and preferences. Okay—jumping off the soapbox now.

I went on a mission to discover the facts that most New Testament scholars agree upon when it comes to textual criticism. What seems to be undisputed is how many manuscripts we have, the general dating of those manuscripts, and how many differences there are between the manuscripts. What scholars disagree on is *what that all means.* But before we get ahead of ourselves, a little history.

Before the printing press was invented, the only way to make copies of books and writings was to do it the old-fashioned way—by hand. In New Testament times, scribes would meticulously copy the eyewitness accounts and letters that were written by the apostles (and in a few cases, those who knew or were close to the apostles). These handwritten copies are called manuscripts. As Christianity grew and spread throughout the Roman Empire, making additional copies of the apostles' writings became increasingly important. After all, Paul couldn't just zip eight hundred miles from Jerusalem to Corinth to preach a sermon every week.

When Paul wrote a letter to a church in his care, he often addressed it to an entire region. For example, the book of Galatians is addressed to "the churches [plural] of Galatia" (1:2). New Testament scholars Dr. Andreas Köstenberger and Dr. Michael Kruger note, "It is unlikely that each of these sub-churches received the *original* letter of Paul; undoubtedly copies were made."[3] In some cases, Paul instructed the local church to read the letter aloud, then send it on to another church (assuming it would be copied) as in Colossians 4:16. So from the get-go, many copies began circulating throughout the known world.

Peach cobbler again
(What is it with this book and peaches?)

To understand how textual criticism works, let's revisit my grandmother's peach cobbler recipe. Can you remember it off the top of your head? Don't jump back to chapter 3, but here's a hint: "cuppa cuppa cuppa." Let's say that my grandmother had the world's worst memory, so she decided to write down the recipe in case she ever forgot the ingredients. Then let's imagine I looked at that original and carefully made my own copy. My three sisters decided they wanted a copy, so I made one for each of them too. Suppose one of my sisters decided to make a few of her own copies from the one I gave her to pass on to her daughters. They, in turn, made copies for their own children, and so on and so on. Within a few generations, there could conceivably be dozens to hundreds of handwritten copies of my nana's recipe.

With her original lost to history or mothballs or whatever, how would someone know whether the copy they had was the same as what my grandmother wrote originally? If only one copy of the recipe existed, there would be no way to know. Maybe someone made a mistake, or misspelled a word, or even worse, intentionally changed one of the ingredients to improve the recipe (can't be done, but thanks for trying). The only way to know if they had an accurate copy

Nana's Peach Cobbler

1 cup self-rising flour
1 cup sugar
1 can peaches, with juice
1 stick batter
Combine first three ingredients.
Slice batter and arrange on top.
Bake at 350° for 30 min

Nana's Peach Cobbler

1 cup self-risi flour
1 cup sugar
1 can peache
1 stick butter

Combine first three ingredients.
Slice butter and arrange on top.
Bake at 350° for 30 minutes

1 cup self-rising flo
1 cup sugar
1 can peache

Nana's Peach Cobbler
1 stick butter
1 can peaches, with juice
1 cup self-rising flour
1 cup sugar

would be to *compare it to the other copies*. In order to do this well, they would want to compare it with as many copies as they could find, and they would generally want the earliest copies possible—the ones closest to the original.

Let's look at several of the copies.

As you can see, among the "manuscripts" of Nana's recipe, there are some differences. It looks like someone misspelled the word *butter* in manuscript 1. Manuscript 2 is hardly readable because it looks like someone spilled coffee all over it. Manuscript 3 seems to be just a torn fragment with only a couple of letters legible. Manuscript 4 has the ingredients in a different order. But if we look at all the manuscripts together, despite the differences between them, it's not very difficult to understand what the recipe says. In fact, *because* there are so many manuscripts that are overall so reliable, it would actually be quite difficult to get the recipe wrong.

The New Testament Evidence

Verifying the New Testament certainly isn't as simple as comparing three differing words on under a dozen manuscripts. The recipe analogy is meant only to show the basic idea of how textual criticism works. With the New Testament, many considerations come into play. Scholars analyze each manuscript with meticulous attention to detail, scribal quality, date, and many other factors.

So how many New Testament manuscripts do we have? According to both conservative and liberal scholars, we have over five thousand manuscripts in Greek, the language in which it was written.[4] How old are they? The earliest manuscript we have is a fragment of the Gospel of John. It's about the size of a credit card and dates to within fifty to one hundred years from the original.[5] I won't bore you with all the details, but it's safe to say that the New Testament has *more* copies and *earlier* copies than *any* work of ancient classical literature.

Here's where things get dicey. Among the thousands of manuscripts we have, there are anywhere from 400,000 to half a million differences, or variants, as scholars call them.[6] I know that seems like a lot, but before you tear up your Bible and use it as kindling for a bonfire, rest assured that most of those variants don't affect the meaning of the text. This is another fact that both Christian and secular scholars agree on. Take, for example, the famously skeptical New Testament scholar Dr. Bart Ehrman, the author of the quote that opened this chapter. He is a former evangelical Christian who became an agnostic and atheist[7] after discovering what he believed to be factual errors in the biblical accounts. He regularly debates evangelical Christian scholars and has appeared on CNN, *The Colbert Report*, and *The Daily Show with Jon Stewart*. He lost his faith, and he's on a mission to explain why we should question our beliefs as well. But *even he* agrees that the bulk of these variants are essentially meaningless. He writes,

> The vast majority of these hundreds of thousands of differences are completely and utterly unimportant and insignificant and don't matter at all. By far the most common differences simply show us that scribes in the ancient world could spell no better

than most people can today (and the scribes didn't have spell-check!). If we really want to know what the apostle Paul had to say about the importance of Jesus' death and resurrection, does it matter to us how he spelled the word "resurrection"? Probably not. Moreover, lots of other kinds of differences in our manuscripts—as we will see—are easy to explain and don't affect the meaning of the writings in the least.[8]

However, as Ehrman goes on to point out, a small percentage of these variants *do* affect the meaning, and we need to be honest about that and deal with it. These are called *meaningful* variants . . . the parts of the text that may or may not be authentic to the original writings.

My Favorite Bible Story That Isn't in the Bible

I'll never forget standing in my kitchen after learning that one of my *favorite* stories in the whole Bible is one of these meaningful variants. I had just opened the fridge to gather ingredients to make sandwiches for the kids as I listened to a class lecture on my computer. I froze when I heard the teacher say that John 7:53–8:11, the beloved story about Jesus saving the life of the woman caught in the act of adultery, was not in the earliest and most reliable manuscripts of the Gospel of John.

I stood by the open refrigerator a moment, stunned. This wasn't something I heard from the progressive pastor. This was something said by the instructor of a New Testament class at a conservative evangelical seminary. But in this case, when the reliability of my Bible was in question, I wasn't about to take anyone's word for it—even if he was a seminary professor with a PhD. I did some research and came upon a well-respected textual critic named Dan Wallace. I began listening to his podcast and stumbled upon an episode entitled, "My Favorite Passage That's Not in the Bible."[9] He agreed that this account in John, the one in which Jesus famously said, "Let him who is without sin cast the first stone" and "Go and sin no more," was not in the earliest and most reliable manuscripts of the Gospel of John. In fact, he demonstrated that the earliest manuscript to include this story is from the fifth century, about four hundred years after the original was written.[10]

How, then, did it find its way into our modern Bibles? It was firmly established in the English Bible through the King James Version, even though it is not found in hundreds of Greek manuscripts. The King James is not a bad translation, but the manuscripts behind it were not the earliest and most reliable. Subsequent translations left the passage in, although in most modern Bibles, it is marked with brackets and a disclaimer. The NIV includes this note: "[The earliest manuscripts and many other ancient witnesses do not have John 7:53-8:11. A few manuscripts include these verses, wholly or in part, after John 7:36, John 21:25, Luke 21:38 or Luke 24:53.]"

The agreement between virtually all New Testament scholars—conservative, liberal, and atheist—is that this section of Scripture is not original to John's Gospel. I realize how mind-blowing this revelation can be. It rattled me so hard that it took me a whole year to process, reason, and think it through. What did this mean for the of the rest of my Bible? Was it trustworthy? Are there other stories in Scripture that I've relied on and believed in that are also not authentic? Did Jesus never really say, "Go and sin no more"? As I reflected on how many sermons have been based on this passage, I was comforted to discover that although most scholars don't recognize this passage as authentic Scripture, some believe the story actually happened. Maybe it was a real event that had been passed down through oral tradition and later added by a scribe so it wouldn't be lost. We can't be sure. But as a student of the Bible and someone committed to its authority, I had to wrestle with this.

The only other significantly long section that most scholars believe is not authentic is Mark 16:9-20. This is referred to as "the long ending of Mark." This is also bracketed and footnoted in most Bibles.

You may have come across other meaningful variants in your Bible reading. For example, have you ever noticed that a verse in one translation of your Bible seems to be shorter (or longer) than that same verse in one of your other Bible translations? These are typically not long passages or entire stories like the two examples above. Most meaningful variants affect only a few words here and there. For example, if you compare Mark 9:29 in the English Standard Version and the New King James Version, you'll find a difference. In this story, Jesus' disciples unsuccessfully attempt to cast a demon out of a young boy. When they ask Jesus why they failed, did he reply, "This kind cannot be driven out by anything but prayer" or

"This kind can come out by nothing but prayer and fasting"? Which is it? Prayer alone, or prayer *and fasting*? It depends on which translation you're reading. There is some debate, but many scholars agree that "and fasting" was not in the original manuscript. Again, this fact is footnoted in most Bibles.

So what did I make of all this? The information seemed overwhelming, but I learned that these meaningful variants are actually quite important. Because we can identify them, we can actually *know* how accurate our copy of the New Testament is. The good news? Our New Testament has been copied with an astounding degree of accuracy. No other work of ancient classical literature even comes close. Here's the really exciting part: Because scholars know what the meaningful variants are, we can be assured that *not one of them* changes any core Christian doctrine. This is also something most scholars agree on. In fact, Dr. Bart Ehrman was questioned on this very issue by Dr. Dan Wallace in a debate about the New Testament in 2008. Even Ehrman agreed that none of these variants bring any cardinal Christian doctrine into question.[11] Thousands of copies from different time periods, theological traditions, and parts of the world *all basically say the same thing*. This is tremendously strong evidence that the New Testament was not, in fact, significantly changed . . . but was copied accurately. (This is the stuff I get excited about.)

We Only Have Error-Ridden Copies?

I purposely began this chapter with a fairly shocking quote from Dr. Bart Ehrman:

> What good is it to say that the autographs (i.e., the
> originals) were inspired? We don't *have* the originals!
> We have only error-ridden copies, and the vast majority
> of these are centuries removed from the originals and
> different from them, evidently, in thousands of ways.[12]

Ehrman is a highly respected academic who knows his stuff. But I want to show you that you don't have to be a Bible scholar to spot his mistake. New Testament scholar Dr. Peter Gurry shared this quote with a group of Christians to see if anyone could recognize the faulty logic. He reported his findings on Twitter, and guess what? It wasn't a pastor or Bible teacher or scholar who found the problem; it was a lawyer—someone trained in logical argumentation and the art of critical thinking.[13] You see, Ehrman can't logically claim that we have error-ridden copies if by his own admission we don't have original writings to compare them with. Remember my soapbox sermon on bias? Despite the fact that there's no evidence that the New Testament has been significantly changed (aside from the variants we know about), he's making an assumption. Because of bias.

Once I learned about textual criticism and how it works, and wrestled through the variants, I was satisfied that the New Testament that sat on my desk accurately reflected what was written almost two thousand years ago. But this wasn't enough. Did the biblical writers get their facts right? In theory, I could be reading a textually reliable story about a religion a bunch of guys made up in the first century.

I could be holding in my hands an accurate copy of *a lie*.

Was It True Only for Them?

The Gospels differ because their writers lived at different times and places and wrote for different reasons decades after Jesus lived. . . . Likely none was an eyewitness.

Peter Enns, *The Bible Tells Me So*

"Who wants to start a new religion?" I asked a feisty group of teenagers during week three of a six-week apologetics class I was teaching to their youth group. After I'd spent an hour pretending to be an atheist and challenging them to defend their faith, they were used to me asking weird questions. One hand shot up, then another. After two more hands were raised, I invited the four boys to join me on the stage.

"Okay. Here are the rules. All four of you are going to conspire to create a brand-new religion that you know is *not true*. You are going to try to convince everyone you know to follow and believe what you say. But before you actually create this pretend religion, I want to ask you a question. Why would you even do that in the first place? What would you have to gain?"

There was a long pause before the first boy raised his hand again. It was obvious he was a leader and well-liked by his peers. Judging by the panda bear onesie he was wearing, he was also a bit of a comedian.

"Money," he deadpanned.

"Okay, good. It certainly makes sense that you could stand to make a lot of money by inventing a religion. You could sell books and merch, take up big offerings, and even afford a healthy salary as a minister. Anyone else? Why would *you* start a fake religion?"

"Maybe . . . to be powerful?" another boy suggested.

"Ah, yes. Power. It could be very tempting to convince people to believe something you know is false if it means they'll hang on every word you say and follow you as an influential leader."

The third boy raised his hand and said, "To be famous."

"Of course!" I replied. "If you were successful, there would be podcasts and YouTube videos and interviews on radio and television. Not to mention celebrity status on social media."

The fourth boy seemed stumped, so I suggested one final motive: girls. "I would imagine that being rich, powerful, and famous would attract a lot of attention from the opposite sex?"

The eyes of all four widened as they giggled a bit, realizing the impact of this last motive. By now, everyone was laughing and probably wondering if these boys were going to leave the meeting and start making plans. But before sending them off to become good little cult leaders, I decided to burst their bubble.

I asked them to imagine what they might do if they

actually *didn't* make any money off their new religion. "In fact, not only is your new religion not profitable, it's actually *costing* you money to spread the news. And not only that, what if you never gained the power and fame you were chasing, but instead got whipped and put in jail for trying to preach your message? And I'm sure you can imagine how attractive the ladies would find a broke, beat-up jailbird."

As they tried to think up reasons to continue spreading their new religion, they were silenced one by one as their expressions fell. When the thought experiment was over, they shuffled back to their seats, deflated. They began to realize what I had come to know after years of studying the historical reliability of the Gospels: The earliest Christians had no possible motivation for making the whole thing up. In fact, they would have had every reason to recant under threat of death and torture. But they didn't.

Because it was all true.

Class Notes

A consistent theme in our class with the progressive pastor was that the earliest Christians represented Christianity in its infancy. The thinking went something like this: We wouldn't expect a brand-new baby to know everything he will know when he's full grown, or to come out of the womb running. First, he must learn to crawl and then to walk. So why would we expect people of a newborn religion to have the same understanding they would have two thousand years later? The pastor explained, "We are more evolved now. The Bible says the Holy Spirit will lead and guide into all truth . . . and that's what he's doing." The implication seemed to be that Paul, Peter, and the other writers of the New Testament represent Christianity in its most primitive form. The Holy Spirit is leading us to do the same work they did . . . to correct wrong doctrines and perceptions. To hear from God in our time.

This made absolutely no sense to me. On the one hand, we *do* see God revealing more about himself throughout the history of the world. Certainly, Moses had more revelation about God than Abraham did. On the other side of the Cross, Paul had a deeper understanding of atonement than the Israelites in the Old Testament did. I would later learn this is what theologians refer to as progressive revelation. It's "progressive" in the sense that God continued to reveal more information to human beings as time went on. But it doesn't mean that the revelation progressed from error to truth. In this way, there is a huge difference between what theologians have historically meant by progressive revelation and what progressive Christians mean. The main difference is that the progressive revelation we find in Scripture never contradicts itself, and the revelation of God culminates in Jesus Christ. As Hebrews 1:1-2 gloriously declares, "Long ago, at many times and in many ways, God spoke to our fathers by the prophets, but in these last days he has spoken to us by his Son, whom he appointed the heir of all things, through whom also he created the world."

In other words, Jesus is God's final word. Progressive revelation is like bricks stacked on top of one another forming a wall of a building. Progressive theology, by contrast, says that we started with the wrong bricks, so we need to remove them and put other ones in—or tear the whole wall down and start over.

While it's true that the disciples of Jesus represent the first Christians, they were also the ones closest to Jesus. They knew him. They walked with him. They learned personally from God in the flesh. For us to assume that we know more about God than they do seemed very arrogant and short-sighted to me.

Once when attempting to articulate these thoughts to the pastor, I said, "But what we find in the Gospels was written by the men who actually knew Jesus . . . the ones who walked with him for three years."

He quickly asked, "How do you know they walked with him?"

"What? Do you think they didn't?" I asked incredulously.

"I'm not saying that. I'm just asking why *you* believe that the people who wrote the Gospels were the ones who actually knew and walked with Jesus."

I had no answer. I was stumped. He told me that the next week we would be learning about "problematic authorship." I had never heard that phrase before, but I already dreaded the next class.

As if I didn't already have more than enough rocks in my shoes, the question "Why do *you* believe the Gospel writers were the ones who walked with Jesus?" had me walking with a limp. *Why do I believe that?* My inner monologue began to chatter. *Surely there is a good reason Christians have believed this for two thousand years. We can't be the first generation to ask this question.*

Once I was convinced that my Bible was faithful to the original manuscripts, I continued my quest. Now I was determined to figure out if the New Testament that sat in my lap was an accurate account of what actually happened in the first century, or if it was simply an accurate copy of a lie. This was not a question the textual critics could answer for me. Now I needed the historians and biblical scholars. I learned that with any work of history, there are certain elements historians look for to help determine whether the work is describing real events or fictional stories. I learned that the New Testament contains an overabundance of these elements, even leading atheist English professor Holly Ordway to change her mind about Christianity. What she once believed was nothing more than a curious superstition she came to understand was real history. She writes,

> I read through the Gospel narratives again, trying
> to take in what they said. . . . I recognized that
> they were historical narratives. I'd been steeped
> in folklore, fantasy, legend, and myth ever since I
> was a child, and had studied these literary genres
> as an adult; I knew their cadences, their flavor,
> their rhythm. None of these stylistic fingerprints
> appeared in the New Testament books that I was
> reading.[1]

Were the Gospel Writers Eyewitnesses?

Some Christian scholars date the Gospels to before the fall of Jerusalem in AD 70, a bit earlier than their secular counterparts. But what they all generally agree on is that they were written by the end of the first century. Even Bart Ehrman points out that most historians date Matthew, Mark, Luke, and John to between AD 65 and 95.[2] As New Testament scholar Peter J. Williams notes, "Mainstream scholars who disbelieve that Jesus was the Messiah nevertheless date the Gospels within the time limits of reliable memory."[3]

The dating suggests not only that the Gospels were written by people who were alive when Jesus was, but also that the books themselves were written with razor-sharp accuracy when it comes to historical details. In his book *Can We Trust the Gospels?*, Williams points out that all four Gospel writers displayed knowledge of local geography, even of places that were quite obscure. Their use of personal names was spot-on with current scholarly research about the popularity and usage of names in that time and place. (Interestingly, the noncanonical Gospels don't come close to that type of accuracy.)[4] The New Testament displays a correct understanding of botanical terms, financial norms, and local languages and customs. Remember, this was a time in history when you couldn't just google that type of information. You had to be there . . . or at least know someone who was. These details certainly don't prove the writers were telling the truth about Jesus, but it certainly helps put to rest the idea that they were random people trying to piece together what had happened from some other geographical location decades in the future. These details point to the writers being eyewitnesses or informed by eyewitnesses.

Well, That's Embarrassing

If there's one thing about human nature I'm sure about, it's that we tend to paint ourselves in the best possible light. Need proof? Click on over to Instagram. Every time I open up my Instagram feed, my senses are assaulted by perfect little families holding hands on perfect little beaches, drinking intricately crafted artisan lattes, cultivating unblemished tomatoes from their immaculately manicured backyard gardens, or enjoying an impeccably lit ice cream date with their well-behaved children. Seeing the barrage of celebrity "no makeup selfies" in all their flawless glory provokes my inner monologue to sarcastically quip, *How brave.*

But I'm not complaining. I much prefer seeing a snapshot of someone's pedicure appointment to witnessing a rehash of the fight they had with their husband that morning (#keepinstagramhappy). But Instagram is not an accurate reflection of history—it's a highlight reel. We humans can't help it. We want to put the best versions of ourselves in the spotlight.

On the contrary, one of the traits of authentic eyewitness testimony that historians look for in ancient writings is called the "criterion of embarrassment." It basically means that one of the ways we can judge whether someone was telling the truth is if they didn't leave out embarrassing details about themselves or their story. In this way, the Gospels are incredibly embarrassing.

Think about the boys whose story I told in the beginning of this chapter. If they were going to make up a religion, would they portray themselves as dim-witted cowards who never seemed to understand what their spiritual guru was talking about? I certainly wouldn't. But here are some ways in which the writers of the New Testament do just that:

- Jesus' disciples never seem to "get" what Jesus is talking about. (Mark 9:32; Luke 18:34; John 12:16)
- They fall asleep three times when Jesus urges them to pray. (Mark 14:32-41)
- They are scolded by Jesus. (Mark 8:33)
- The apostles fiercely disagree with each other. (Galatians 2:11)
- The disciples run away and hide like cowards when Jesus is arrested. (Mark 14:50-52)
- They disown Jesus when asked if they know him. (Matthew 26:33-35, 69-75)
- Both Jewish leaders and Jesus' disciples constantly doubt him. (Matthew 12:39-41; 17:9, 22-23; 28:16-17; Mark 16:14; John 2:18-22)

The Gospel writers also weren't afraid to break convention and even invite ridicule by relying on the word of women as evidence for one of the greatest miracles in history:

- All four Gospels record that women were the first witnesses of Jesus' resurrection. This is embarrassing because back then, the testimony of women wasn't even admissible in court.[5] (Matthew 28; Mark 16; Luke 24; John 20)

The Gospel writers also included many demanding sayings of Jesus and difficult details of his life. Remember when Jesus told everyone they would have to eat his body and drink his blood? I might have left that out if I were trying to make my new religion appeal to the masses. The Gospel writers record Jesus calling people "enemies" (Matthew 5:44), "pagans" (Matthew 5:47, NIV), "hypocrites" (Matthew 6:2), "thieves" (Matthew 6:20), "dogs" and "pigs" (Matthew 7:6), "false prophets" (Matthew 7:15), "a wicked and adulterous generation" (Matthew 12:39, NIV), "blind guides" (Matthew 15:14), "defiled," (Matthew 15:18), "fools" (Matthew 23:17), "whitewashed tombs" (Matthew 23:27), "serpents" and a "brood of vipers" (Matthew 23:33), and "cursed" (Matthew 25:41) . . . and that's just from Matthew's Gospel alone.

If I were going to try to peddle my new belief system to as many people as possible, I might not include the fact that Jesus' own family called him crazy (Mark 3:20-21) or that others called him a "drunkard" (Matthew 11:19) and "raving mad" (John 10:20, NIV). For my mostly Jewish audience, I would certainly not have the central figure of my new religion be crucified—when my own Holy Book says that anyone who is crucified is cursed (Deuteronomy 21:23). It would be like saying, "Hey, worship this guy . . . he's cursed!" The truth is that you simply wouldn't add these details if they weren't true.

If the gospel was fabricated by a bunch of first-century Jewish men, their tendency would be to simplify, unify, clarify, and beautify Jesus' sayings—to make Christianity much broader, easier, and more pleasant. But they didn't because it's not broad, easy, or pleasant. It's incredibly difficult. It's described as a narrow road that few people actually find (Matthew 7:13-14).

In my quest to discover if the historic claims of Christianity were true, it was important to make a distinction. Before I could evaluate whether I thought the Bible is inerrant and inspired, I needed to know if the *gospel* is true. And for this, I simply needed reliable eyewitness testimony.

Class Notes

I had been reassured to discover that the Gospels accurately portrayed the first-century Middle Eastern world while not shying away from disclosing embarrassing details about Jesus' life and followers. Both suggested that they are trustworthy accounts. Yet I was bothered by one more question: Why do we find so many differing details in the Gospel accounts? Is it because the writers weren't who the church historically believed them to be? Were they just a bunch of random guys who lived decades after Jesus' life and wrote in different places for different reasons? If they were, how did they write with such pointed accuracy? Considering what I had already discovered, this seemed a bit far-fetched. But why were there differences in the first place?

In class one day, the progressive pastor walked us through a few of these supposed contradictions. "Were there two donkeys involved in Jesus' Triumphal Entry into Jerusalem as Matthew reports, or was there one, as Mark, Luke, and John record?" he asked. "At Jesus' resurrection, was there one angel as Matthew and Mark mention, or two as Luke and John describe?" He observed that often Christians read through an entire Gospel, and by the time they get to the next one, they don't tend to notice the differences in the same stories because they aren't reading the stories side by side. He asked if anyone had ever actually read them that way, and I raised my hand to indicate that I had.

"What did you make of the differences?" he inquired.

"Well, I suppose I didn't notice very many," I said, "but the ones I saw didn't bother me. Regarding the number of donkeys, I just figured that Matthew was standing at a different angle than John, or that he didn't feel the need to mention the second donkey. It's not like he said there was only one," I improvised.

Questions surrounding biblical accuracy have both delighted skeptics and troubled Christians for many years. In fact, so much intellectual consideration has been given to the subject that thousands of pages of scholarly treatises have been compiled into tomes for the curious to peruse. Ultimately, these so-called "contradictions" can be resolved, but there's a bigger question underneath these queries: Can we trust the testimony of the four Gospels?

This is a question that left J. Warner Wallace largely untroubled. As a homicide detective, he is trained to know when someone is telling the truth. His job requires him to have certain expertise in the area of eyewitness testimony. In his book *Cold Case Christianity*, he recounts being called to a crime scene in which all four eyewitnesses sat together in the back of a police car while they waited for him to arrive at the scene. He wrote that this nearly ruined the case. Why? Because when eyewitnesses have a chance to talk with each other, compare notes, and share observations, they will inevitably harmonize their stories. This is a surefire sign that key details essential to solving the case are probably being left out or smoothed over.

Wallace reports that when eyewitnesses are separated from one another, "they are far more likely to provide an uninfluenced, pure account of what they saw."[6] He writes that he actually *expects* authentic testimonies to differ from one another because each eyewitness has a unique perspective, worldview, and life experience. This is why, when he investigated a robbery at a small grocery store, he was able to solve the case even though the two eyewitnesses differed significantly on key details.

One was a thirty-eight-year-old woman who was an interior designer. She reported that the robber was wearing an Izod polo shirt and made no mention of him having a gun. The other eyewitness was an unmarried twenty-three-year-old male plumber. He said that the robber had a Ruger P95 9mm handgun and might have been wearing a T-shirt. They offered other differing details as well, so Wallace wondered if they were describing two entirely different crimes. It turns out that the woman was standing behind the robber and never saw a gun. She noticed his polo because as a designer, she was trained to notice those types of details, plus she had just bought a similar shirt for her husband. The man (who was less attentive to fashion) was standing in front of and facing the robber. Because of his vantage point, he spotted the weapon and immediately recognized it as a Ruger P95 because his father owned an identical handgun.

After piecing together what actually happened, Wallace noted,

> Every case I handle is like this; witnesses seldom agree on every detail. In fact, when two people agree completely on every detail of their account, I am inclined to believe that they have either contaminated each other's observations or are working together to pull the wool over my eyes. I expect truthful, reliable eyewitnesses to disagree along the way.[7]

This is why when, as a committed atheist, Wallace read the Gospel accounts, he wasn't bothered by the differences. In fact, if he was troubled by anything, it was that what he found in the pages of Matthew, Mark, Luke, and John were the characteristics of authentic eyewitness testimony he had been trained as a detective to recognize. This was one of the pieces of evidence that would eventually lead him to faith in Christ.

He concluded what I concluded. The Gospel writers were reliable eyewitnesses of the events of Jesus' life. Yet each wrote from a different perspective and with a different audience in mind. Take Matthew, for example. He was writing his Gospel to a Jewish audience and naturally included details relevant to Old Testament prophecy regarding Jesus as the Jewish Messiah.[8] This is why it might have been important to him to mention the second donkey at the Triumphal Entry. A prophecy from Zechariah 9:9 tells us that the Messiah would ride into Jerusalem "on a donkey, on a colt, the foal of a donkey." A colt is a young male that is still dependent on its mother, which is why Matthew records the two donkeys being found together. This was an important detail for Matthew as he was demonstrating how Jesus fulfilled the Jewish prophecy.

Mark, on the other hand, was writing to the broader Roman audience. He didn't tend to include details that were specifically Jewish because his audience wouldn't have found that information necessary. Luke was an immaculate historian who interviewed the eyewitnesses to compile "an orderly account" for the literate and scholarly of the Gentile world (Luke 1:1-4). Mark and Luke would not have needed to include the fact that the second donkey (the mother) was present because it would have had no significance to their audience.

John, writing a bit later, seemed more concerned with the theological implications of the events of Jesus' life than chronology or historical details. In fact, around AD 200, Clement of Alexandria tells us, "But, last of all, John, perceiving that the external facts had been made plain in the Gospel, being urged by his friends, and inspired by the Spirit, composed a spiritual Gospel."[9] John's Gospel simply says, "Jesus found a young donkey and sat on it." John expected the reader to be familiar with the narratives in Matthew, Mark, and Luke, so he compressed the details as much as possible in order to get to the theological significance of this event.

Now for the question I know is burning in every reader's

mind: How many donkeys were there? Neither Mark nor Luke nor John state that there was *only* one donkey. Put simply, there were two, and Matthew was the only one who recorded the second.[10] Of course, this is just one of many such differences, but I offer it to show how much work goes into truly seeking to understand a book that was written in a culture, era, and place that is entirely foreign to most of us.

When confronted with these conflicts, I could have simply said, "Matthew says it's two donkeys, and Mark says one. It's all lies. I'm out." I could have given up. Instead, like a starving man in a desert, I consumed book after book and lecture after lecture. I was hungry for truth, and the one place I had always gone to find truth was being cross-examined. The bottom line was that I needed to find out what was true . . . whatever it was. But seeking and searching is hard work. I've heard it said that a little bit of knowledge will make you an atheist, but a lot of knowledge will make you a Christian. I have found this to be true. Loads of volumes have been written on the reliability of the New Testament. If the doubter will keep reading—keep searching, keep digging—the truth will come out.

It takes work, and the hungry doubter will do the work.

"Ask Me Anything"

"Ask me anything. I can tell you're a bit anxious about what we've been learning in class," the progressive pastor told me.

On this particular afternoon, I wasn't entirely sure why I had even picked up the phone to call him. Part of me hoped our conversation would culminate with me saying, "Thanks for the invitation, but this class isn't for me." It was early enough in the process that I wouldn't have caused a stir by leaving quietly, like a college student dropping a class in the first few weeks of the semester. No big deal.

But as he had warned us in one of the first meetings, I had now read and heard things I would never be able to unknow. And with my truth-seeking nature, it would be next to impossible for me to leave all those questions hanging in the air. Plus, I had read a troubling statement about the deity of Jesus in one of the books we'd been reading. After bringing that up, I rambled on about not being on the same page with everyone else in class and wondering why we were reading this particular book. He broke in: "I just wanted to let you know that if you're uncomfortable with something, just ask. I promise to answer any question honestly. If there's one thing I know, it's that the gospel can stand up to scrutiny. There's nothing to be afraid of."

I was instantly set as ease. *See, he does believe in the gospel. Maybe he's just trying to push us so we will come out at the end standing even stronger in our convictions*, I thought to myself. He was right. I had been beating around the bush. I needed to be more direct about what I really wanted to know.

I mustered some courage and spit out, "Do you believe the Bible is divinely inspired? Do you believe in hell?"

"Yes. I believe the Bible is divinely inspired, and I believe in hell. I don't believe Hitler woke up in heaven right after he died. Absolutely yes to both questions."

"Okay," I said, smiling with relief. "I think that gives me enough of what I need to know right now. Thank you."

I have no idea why those specific two questions had popped into my mind in that moment. Maybe it was because you can't really have a rational discussion about the deity of Jesus unless you believe the Bible is God's Word. Perhaps it was because none of it would even matter if hell didn't exist. If everyone is going to heaven, what is the point of having any kind of conversation around the finer theological points? Just live and let live. It will all work out in the end.

But my relief was short-lived—because words matter. Words like *hell*, *divine*, and *inspired* can mean different things to different people. I would later learn that what he meant and what I meant when we used those same words could not have been more at odds. And when it comes to the way we talk about the Bible, I was about to discover how true it is that the devil is in the details.

9

Authority Problems

*The church will continue to be even more irrelevant
when it quotes letters from 2,000 years ago
as their best defense.*

Rob Bell

I could predict with fairly certain accuracy what I would be
feeling as I walked into class on any given day. I would pull
into the parking lot, rehearse my arguments, step out of my
car, and give myself a pep talk. My inner monologue went
something like this: *Okay, Childers. Be strong. Speak the truth.
You know what he's teaching is wrong, and you've thought and
prayed all week to come up with your points. You've got this.
Don't back down.* And with fired-up confidence, I would
walk into the classroom, see my classmates, and instantly
(cue Debbie Downer music) back down. Every last flame of
fortitude would be snuffed out when my inner monologue,
which had been incredibly helpful just moments before,
would suddenly punk out on me and start sniveling, *Oh, just*

look at all their faces. They are so loving and nice. They are just trying to figure things out. He's just trying to figure things out. Stop being so judgmental. You're probably the one who's wrong.

Then within minutes I would realize that whatever answer I'd come up with for the questions from last week's class were irrelevant anyway, because everyone had moved on to the shiny new skeptical controversy du jour.

At some point it finally hit me: For the pastor and my classmates, the questions mattered more than the answers. It didn't really seem like anyone was interested in researching facts or reaching conclusions. They seemed way more excited about landing on the next question—and the more controversial, the better. Because I am a truth-driven person, this was like my own personal custom-crafted hell.

Usually I felt as if I were on an emotional teeter-totter during class, but in one of the last sessions I attended, I was feeling a bit stronger. I knew I wouldn't stay in it much longer, and I was feeling feisty. The progressive pastor asked the group a question about the Bible: "Do you think these writers were actually inspired by God, or were they just writing the best they knew how?"

Recalling my conversation with him about whether Scripture was inspired by God, I stopped him. "Wait a minute. You told me yourself that you believe the Bible is divinely inspired. Can you explain what you're asking?" (One life lesson I learned in this class is that some questions are really just answers masquerading as questions.)

His eyes became like dinner plates, and he went silent. Looking down at the top of the white folding table where he was seated, he remained silent as others made a few passing comments. After a couple of moments, he looked up and said, "A few minutes ago I asked a question . . . and I want to clarify. When I say that the Bible is 'divinely inspired,' I mean that it's inspired on the same level as something written by A. W. Tozer or C. S. Lewis . . . or perhaps one of my sermons on Sunday. It's inspired, but maybe not in the way that word is typically used."

I could not believe what I was hearing. He knew exactly what I'd been asking when I inquired about his views on inspiration months before. He had redefined the word (without letting me know) and given me the answer he thought I wanted to hear. But I hadn't wanted to hear a particular answer. I'd wanted the truth.

How Do Progressives View the Bible?

Make no mistake, just like historic Christians, progressives find Scripture compelling. The difference is that, rather than viewing it as the authoritative Word from God to people, they see the Bible as an antiquated library of books that we can examine like ancient relics. In their view, the Bible is our spiritual ancestors' best attempts to understand God in their own cultures, using whatever knowledge they had at the time. Because humans now have a higher and wiser view of God, progressives believe we can now read the Bible the way it is meant to be read—not as the authoritative word of God, but as our predecessors' spiritual travel journal.

Biblical scholar and progressive thought leader Peter Enns

writes extensively from this viewpoint. In his book *The Bible Tells Me So: Why Defending Scripture Has Made Us Unable to Read It*, Enns talks about how he became serious about the Bible after graduating from a Christian college and feeling humiliated after witnessing a debate between two friends: a "smart atheist" and a "smart Christian." Realizing that he hadn't intellectually thought through this "Jesus thing,"[1] Enns defines this debate as a turning point. He went on to read the entire Bible several times, along with books on theology, church history, and philosophy. After earning a seminary degree in Old Testament studies, he went on to Harvard, where he received a PhD in Near Eastern Languages and Civilizations. Enns is no Bible ignoramus.

After reading modern liberal scholarship and becoming persuaded that he just couldn't make the Bible behave anymore, he reached a final turning point during a lecture given by a Jewish rabbi. The professor was trying to make sense of the scene in the desert when Moses struck the rock and water gushed out. This happened twice, forty years apart during the Israelites' trek in the wilderness, leading the careful reader to wonder how they got water in between the two rock-striking incidents. The rabbi explained that some ancient Jewish scholars came up with the idea that the rock must have simply followed the Israelites around the wilderness like some kind of "movable drinking fountain."[2] For Enns, that sounded a little out there, but he wasn't that bothered by it because it reflected Jewish rather than Christian thought—until the rabbi had the class turn to 1 Corinthians 10:4, where the apostle Paul seemed to be in agreement.

Enns writes,

> In 1 Corinthians 10:4, the apostle Paul mentions—as
> if it's no big deal and everyone's on board—this *very
> same idea* of a rock following the Israelites around
> in the desert supplying water. He writes, "For they
> drank from the spiritual *rock that followed them*, and
> the rock was Christ." And not only was there a rock in
> the desert tagging along with Moses, but the rock,
> Paul says, was Jesus. . . .
>   I felt like I was watching my whole view of the
> Bible collapse like a house of cards—there one
> minute, familiar and looking stable, and then gone
> the next minute with a good stiff wind.[3]

Now that the rabbi had ventured into Enns's own backyard
(the New Testament), his view of the Bible was left deeply
shaken. Enns was troubled by the fact that, when commenting on an Old Testament passage, Paul didn't appear to be
following the grammatical-historical rule of biblical interpretation he'd learned in seminary. If Paul was inspired by
God to write Scripture, why would he go "off script" and
incorporate a strange Jewish legend into his commentary?

But Enns doesn't mention the sentence that directly pre-
cedes the one he quotes: "All ate the same spiritual food, and
all drank the same spiritual drink" (1 Corinthians 10:3-4).
Spiritual drink. Paul isn't saying that a physical rock followed
the Israelites around but rather that the rock *symbolized* Jesus
. . . and gave them *spiritual* food and water.

Nonetheless, Enns describes this as "the straw that broke the camel's back."[4] He concluded that, rather than speaking for God, the words the biblical writers wrote about God's nature, actions, and decrees may have been just their own sincere opinions based on the world in which they lived. As a celebrated scholar in the progressive movement and someone Rachel Held Evans described as a "mentor,"[5] Enns's influence on progressive thought about the Bible cannot be overstated.

Limited

Pete Enns writes that "the Bible—from back to front—is the story of God told from the limited point of view of real people living at a certain place and time." His approach to reading the Bible can best be summed up in his own words:

> The Bible is an ancient book and we shouldn't be surprised to see it act like one. So seeing God portrayed as a violent, tribal warrior is not how God is but how he was understood to be by the ancient Israelites communing with God in their time and place.[6]

Progressive Christian pioneer Brian McLaren puts it like this:

> Human beings can't do better than their very best at any given moment to communicate about God as they understand God, and . . . Scripture faithfully reveals the evolution of our ancestors'

best attempts to communicate their successive best understandings of God. As human capacity grows to conceive of a higher and wiser view of God, each new vision is faithfully preserved in Scripture like fossils in layers of sediment.[7]

Progressive pastor and theologian Brian Zahnd writes,

The Old Testament is the inspired telling of the story of Israel coming to know their God. It's a process. God doesn't evolve, but Israel's understanding of God obviously does. . . . It seems obvious that we should accept that as Israel was in the process of receiving the revelation of Yahweh, some unavoidable assumptions were made. One of the assumptions was that Yahweh shared the violent attributes of other deities worshiped in the ancient Near East. These assumptions were inevitable, but they were wrong.[8]

Franciscan friar and progressive favorite Richard Rohr writes,

The Jewish Scriptures, which are full of anecdotes of destiny, failure, sin, and grace, *offer almost no self-evident philosophical or theological conclusions that are always true.* . . . We even have four, often conflicting versions of the life of Jesus in Matthew, Mark, Luke, and John. There is not one clear theology of God, Jesus, or history presented, despite our attempt to pretend there is.[9]

According to progressive wisdom, the prophets Christians have always believed were speaking for God weren't really speaking for him. They were simply doing their best to communicate what they believed about God in the times and places in which they lived. So you know when God tells Moses to drive the Canaanites out of the Promised Land, destroy them, smash their altars, and burn their idols (Deuteronomy 7:1-6)? According to progressive interpretations, that wasn't necessarily God. That was probably just Moses speaking what he *thought* God was saying. Remember that time when God told Ezekiel to lie on his side for 430 days (Ezekiel 4:4-8)? Probably not God. When God supposedly told Isaiah to walk around naked and barefoot for three years (Isaiah 20:1-6)? That was probably just what Isaiah *thought* God wanted him to do.

But reading the Bible this way brings up a whole slew of questions. If the prophets got God's word wrong . . . how can we know which parts of the Bible are actually his Word? If the prophets got God's word wrong, at best they were ignorant—at worst they were liars and frauds. It doesn't take a biblical scholar to recognize how this way of thinking irredeemably undermines the concepts of biblical inspiration and authority. It doesn't take a trained theologian to see how this puts the Bible under the authority of the reader rather than the reader standing under the authority of God's Word.

Subjective

In Rob Bell's book *What Is the Bible? How an Ancient Library of Poems, Letters, and Stories Can Transform the Way You Think and Feel about Everything,* Bell devotes an entire chapter to the issue of biblical authority. He argues that when Christians talk about "authority," they are really just assigning it to someone who has told them what the Bible says and means. In other words, we aren't really giving authority to the Bible but to its interpreters. He writes,

> They were taught by their pastor or parents or authority figures to submit to the authority of the Bible, but *that's impossible to do without submitting first to whoever is deciding what the Bible is even saying.* . . . The problem, of course, is that the folks who talk the most about the authority of the Bible also seem to talk the most about things like objective and absolute truth, truth that exists *independent of relational realities.*[10]

He's right about one thing: People who believe in biblical authority do emphasize absolute truth—truth that exists independent of relational realities. Remember bacon? (I guess I'm one of those "folks.") Our *perception* of how bacon will impact our bodies might be affected by what experts (and some nonexperts) tell us about it, but the truth will bear out in actual reality—despite what we may earnestly believe or not believe. The goal should be to correct wrong perceptions and beliefs that may have been passed down by others. In the same way, a good student of the Bible will seek to understand what the Bible is saying and to interpret it properly, even if it goes against their "relational realities."

On the one hand, Rob Bell has a point. Even the most conservative Christian is conceding to a certain "relational reality" in believing in the inspiration and authority of the Scriptures. We have a long church history of generally agreed-upon beliefs about the Bible, and as someone who is trying to get to the bottom of historic Christianity, I agree those beliefs bear some weight. Although believers have argued about interpretations like crazy throughout church history, one thing has always been agreed upon by historic Christians: The Bible—*the whole Bible*—is God's Word, inspired by God and authoritative for our lives. We believe this because of good philosophy, logic, and arguments that demonstrate it to be the case. But there's also a relational reality that can't be ignored or downplayed: the historic witness.

As I first considered Bell's argument, I thought, *But wait a minute! Isn't Bell's view also shaped by relational realities?* In other words, aren't he and the other progressive voices quoted in this chapter all influenced by different voices in culture when they redefine what the Bible is and how much authority it holds for their lives?

A perfect example of the undermining of the concept of biblical inspiration and authority comes from progressive Lutheran minister Nadia Bolz-Weber's book *Shameless: A Sexual Reformation.* Bolz-Weber argues that the view of sexuality and gender Christians have held for two thousand years needs a serious overhaul. She believes that teaching young people to wait to have sex until they are married can be harmful and repress their sexual flourishing. Along with affirming same-sex relationships, gender nonconformity, abortion, and even moderate pornography consumption, Bolz-Weber isn't just suggesting that we make a few amendments to our Christian sexual ethic. She writes, "I'm saying let's burn it the f*** down and start over."[11]

Her book isn't primarily about the Bible, but in order to teach this new view of sexuality, she has to redefine biblical authority and how the Bible is to be read and interpreted. Bolz-Weber tells the story of one of her parishioners, a lesbian, who claims to have found sexual healing at a Lakota sweat lodge retreat. Standing in front of the firepit, the woman tore eight pages out of her Bible—the ones that directly address homosexuality. One by one she threw them into the flames, setting herself free from their edicts and from the rigid church environment in which she grew up. Then she tore out the four Gospels, clutched them to her heart, and heaved the rest of her Bible into the fire. Bolz-Weber explains:

> There are those who will say that it is "dangerous" to think we can decide for ourselves what is sacred in the Bible and what is not. I reject this idea, and here's why. The Gospels are the canon within the canon. . . . The point of gravity is the story of Jesus, the Gospel. The closer a text of the Bible is to that story or to the heart of that story's message, the more authority it has. The farther away it is, the less its authority.[12]

This statement reveals that Bolz-Weber does not believe the entire Bible is equally authoritative or inspired. If certain parts are more "sacred" than others, this leaves the reader in the position of deciding which parts to obey and which parts to throw out.

Richard Rohr states it even more plainly when he explains what he calls the "Jesus hermeneutic":

> Just interpret Scripture the way that Jesus did!
> He ignores, denies, or openly opposes his own
> Scriptures whenever they are imperialistic, punitive,
> exclusionary, or tribal.[13]

As you'll soon discover, I disagree that Jesus ever ignored or opposed the Scripture. Furthermore, if we treat Scripture this way, we effectively make the reader the authoritative standard for what is true. With a Bible remade in our own image, we are no longer obeying God; instead we're following our own thoughts, feelings, and preferences.

So I suppose the question is this: Which relational reality will we appeal to when deciding our view? Our own darkened hearts following the culture around us? Or should we take a cue from those who lived closest to Jesus—or maybe take a cue from Jesus himself?

What Was Jesus' View of Scripture?

When I first heard of these new (to me at least) ways of reading and understanding the Bible, Rob Bell would have been right on the money about me. I believed Scripture was authoritative because that's what I was told to believe. It's what I was taught at my private Christian schools, my evangelical churches, and by my Bible-believing parents. These were the relationships that shaped my reality. But when I began to study these issues for myself, it wasn't enough to feel confident that the Bible sitting in my lap was the same thing that was originally written . . . or even that the writers told the truth. Even if both of those questions passed the test (and I hope the last two chapters have demonstrated that they have), I needed to answer the burning question, *Is the Bible the Word of God?*

When I asked myself this, I realized there is no way to scientifically prove that the Bible is God's Word. Even if God himself appeared in the sky and declared, "The Bible is my Word!" there would still be skeptics who would explain it away. Also, 1 Corinthians 2:14 tells us that "people who aren't spiritual can't receive these truths from God's Spirit" (NLT). If that's true, then we should expect many people to deny that the Bible is God's Word. So where did this leave me? Is this belief nothing but a blind leap of faith, or just some kind of feeling I have in my heart? I suggest that it's not, and here's why.

If the Bible is reliable both in text and in eyewitness testimony, then I have good reason to trust what it says *about Jesus*. I have good reason to believe that what it records Jesus saying and teaching is accurate. And according to the four Gospels, Jesus has quite a bit to say about Scripture. In the famous Sermon on the Mount, Jesus taught that rather than coming to abolish the Law and the Prophets, he came to fulfill them (Matthew 5:17). The Jewish "Law and the Prophets" contain the same books as what we call the Old Testament. Later in Matthew's Gospel, Jesus gives a fairly unpleasant rebuke of the Pharisees, whom he called a brood of vipers. After predicting that they would persecute, scourge, and even kill some of the prophets Jesus would send, he pronounces this judgment:

> That on you may come all the righteous blood shed on earth, from the blood of righteous Abel to the blood of Zechariah the son of Barachiah, whom you murdered between the sanctuary and the altar. Truly, I say to you, all these things will come upon this generation.
>
> MATTHEW 23:35-36

Although the Jewish Law and the Prophets contain the same books as our Old Testament, they are placed in a different order. In the Jewish Scriptures, Abel was killed in the first book, Genesis, and Zechariah was killed in the last, Chronicles. So in sealing the fate of the Pharisees, *Jesus was also affirming the entire Old Testament as Scripture.*

Authoritative

When I was in my early twenties, I tried to fast for seven whole days. Seven. Days. Day one was a piece of cake (without the cake, of course). But after feeling light-headed on day two, I reasoned that if I turned it into a "liquid fast," it would still count. So I drank some carrot juice. By day three my resolve had become about as fluid as the juice, so

166

I added some protein powder. By day four, I was practically putting entire meals into the blender so they would qualify as "liquid." My seven-day fast was a big fat fail.

I can't imagine what it was like for Jesus to spend forty days in the dusty and rocky desert, the only other soul he might meet being a criminal or a hungry beast. By the time the devil showed up, Jesus hadn't eaten for forty days, and he was hungry. "If you are the Son of God, tell this stone to become bread," the enemy taunted. The devil knew Jesus was the Son of God. In fact, Colossians 1:16 tells us that all things were made by him and for him. Imagine the irony of a created being saying to his Creator, "If you are the Son of God, tell this stone to become bread."

As the Creator of the universe, Jesus could have called a legion of angels to his side to banish the devil. He could have simply waved his hand and sent the devil flying. But this is not how Jesus chose to fight. Jesus fought using the *authority* of the Scriptures. Quoting Deuteronomy 8:3, Jesus said, "It is written, 'Man shall not live by bread alone, but by every word that comes from the mouth of God.'" The devil tempted him two more times, and each time Jesus began his answer by saying, "It is written . . ."

What blows my mind about this dialogue is that the devil quoted Scripture back to Jesus! After taking Jesus to the top of the Temple in Jerusalem, the devil suggested he jump. "It is written," Satan said, quoting from Psalm 91, "'he will command his angels concerning you,' and 'On their hands they will bear you up, lest you strike your foot against a stone.'" Imagine that. The devil quoted the Scripture correctly but *twisted its meaning*. This wasn't just a battle over *what* was written; it was a battle over *interpretation*. But Jesus wasn't having it. Rather than engage in a lengthy debate about hermeneutics, Jesus replied, "It is written," once again. Bible scholar Andrew Wilson comments on this passage:

> He [Jesus] has the resources of heaven available, yet he fights by using the authority of the Scriptures. . . . His position is unequivocal: "You're trying to tempt me, but the Scriptures have spoken. That's the end of the conversation."[14]

Inspired

One day Jesus was teaching a large crowd in the Temple courts where some Pharisees were gathered. In a brilliant exchange, Jesus appealed to the *inspiration* of Scripture to help them understand that the Messiah is more than just a descendant of David. He said, "How is it then that David, *speaking by the Spirit*, called him [the Messiah] 'Lord'?"[15] This is where we get our very definition of divine inspiration—from Jesus himself.

The historic understanding of the word *inspiration* as it applies to Scripture is that God literally "breathed out" his Word through humans. We certainly see their personalities, cultures, and writing styles reflected (they weren't human typewriters), but God used them as vehicles to put his words on the page. Thus, it wasn't the writers *themselves* who were inspired, but the words they wrote in the Bible. Second Timothy 3:16-17 says, "All Scripture is breathed out by God and profitable for teaching, for reproof, for correction, and for training in righteousness, that the man of God may be complete, equipped for every good work." The phrase "breathed out by God" comes from one single Greek word that suggests Scripture is the very breath of God himself. Dr. Michael Kruger writes, "This suggests the absolute highest authority for Scripture, the authority of the divine voice."[16]

As Kruger points out, the authority and inspiration of Scripture are closely connected. Whenever Jesus said, "It is written," he wasn't appealing just to authority but also to inspiration. In his book *Christ and the Bible*, theologian and Bible scholar John Wenham wrote, "It is . . . clear that Jesus understood 'It is written' to be equivalent to 'God says.'"[17] In fact, Jesus and his apostles quote the Old Testament by using the phrase "it is written" (or its equivalent) dozens of times in the New Testament. In other words, what God says, goes. If the Bible is God's inspired Word, which Jesus surely seemed to believe, it has the authority to correct our thinking and behavior—and not the other way around.

The Word of God

But we don't have to rely on statements like "it is written" and "speaking by the Spirit" to discern what Jesus thought the Scripture was. Over and over again, he stated *explicitly* that it is the *very word of God*. When the Pharisees were trying to trip him up in Matthew 15, he answered by referencing several commands from Exodus, Leviticus, and Deuteronomy, saying, "For God commanded . . ." (Matthew 15:4). Notice he didn't say, "The Scripture commands" or "Our Holy book says" or "Your scribes wrote." No. It was, "God commanded." Later in Matthew 22:31, he quoted Exodus 3:6, saying, "Have you not read *what was said to you by God . . .*" (emphasis mine). In Mark 7:8-13, he criticized the Pharisees for leaving "the commandment of God" and adding their own traditions to Scripture. He told them that they "void the *word of God* by [their] tradition" (emphasis mine).

It's clear that Jesus didn't see Scripture as simply a human cultural product—*he saw it as the inspired and authoritative Word of God.*

But what about the books in the New Testament? Of course, when Jesus was quoting Scripture, the New Testament hadn't been written yet. But Jesus made two powerful statements to his disciples when they were gathered together just before his crucifixion:

> These things I have spoken to you while I am still with you. But the Helper, the Holy Spirit, whom the Father will send in my name, he will teach you all things and bring to your remembrance all that I have said to you.
>
> JOHN 14:25-26

And:

> I still have many things to say to you, but you cannot bear them now. When the Spirit of truth comes, he will guide you into all the truth, for he will not speak

on his own authority, but whatever he hears he will
speak, and he will declare to you the things that are
to come.

JOHN 16:12-13

With these statements, Jesus was predicting and promising
that the Holy Spirit would speak through his apostles to give
the final revelation of God to humans—our New Testament.
From the time the Gospels and the letters of Paul were written, Christians recognized them to be Scripture, carrying the
same authority and divine inspiration as the Old Testament.[18]

Class Notes

"I just don't understand why so many Christians worship
the Bible. It's like they think it's the third member of the
Trinity or something. Sounds like bibliolatry to me," someone quipped in class one day.

I was so confused. *Do people really think that if you believe
the Bible is authoritative, you must be worshiping it?* I raised my
index finger to signal I had something to say. "If we believe
the Bible is God's Word, doing what it says it isn't bibliolatry.
It's called obedience," I said. "I mean . . . the Bible didn't die
on the cross for my sins. Jesus did. But the Bible is where I
get my information about Jesus. They go hand in hand."

I had the hardest time understanding why people would
equate a belief in biblical authority with idol worship. It
wasn't until years later that I began to figure out that, not
only did progressives buy into the misconception that

Christians worship the Bible, they criticized those Christians they believed approached the Bible as a rule book. Pete Enns seems to suggest that Christians tend to check their brains at the door when reading the Bible, by accepting it as a "seamless, smooth, problem-free, legal brief."[19] I have never personally met a Christian who would describe it this way, nor have I come across any scholarly books that characterize Scripture in such simplistic terms. On the contrary, I have come across multiple thousands of written pages that dig deep into the weeds of subjects like coherence, Bible difficulties, and common misconceptions, such as viewing the Bible in its entirety as a legal brief.

Even so, Brian McLaren calls this the "constitutional approach."[20] He says,

> Like lawyers, we look for precedents in past cases of interpretation, sometimes favoring older interpretations as precedents, sometimes asserting newer ones have rendered the old ones obsolete. We seek to distinguish "spirit" from "letter" and argue the "framers' intent," seldom questioning whether the passage in question was actually intended by the original authors and editors to be a universal, eternally binding law.[21]

He argues that reading the Bible this way makes it possible to justify just about anything. To prove his point, he asks the question, "How should we treat our enemies?" and directs the reader's attention to some New Testament verses that say we should love our enemies, do good to them, and never seek revenge. Next he points to some Old Testament verses that he suggests tell us to joyfully dash our enemies' infants against rocks, hate them, and utterly destroy them. So which is it?

He presents several different methods Christian scholars have used to deal with this tension. Without offering any references to back up his claims, he writes,

> Some say "first mention" is primary. Others say that last mention trumps first mention. Some say the Old Testament is valid unless the New Testament overturns the Old Testament. Others say, no, it's a *new* Testament, so it doesn't depend on the old, but replaces it. Some say the Bible permits whatever it doesn't forbid, and others say it forbids whatever it doesn't permit. Some say, "Interpret Scripture with Scripture," but they never quite make it clear which Scripture trumps the other.[22]

I spent years reading scholars of all types and never encountered *even one* who suggested any of these proposed solutions (at least in the same way McLaren implies). These may be common interpretive mistakes made by otherwise well-meaning Christians, but I don't think you'll find an accredited seminary today that would teach hermeneutics this way. It's true that scholars encourage Bible readers to allow Scripture to interpret Scripture, but that doesn't mean you decide which one "trumps the other."

In fact, what was taught repetitiously (even annoyingly so) in every seminary class I audited was that we must approach the Bible with good grammar by recognizing cultural idioms, figures of speech, and genre. We also learned to recognize *descriptive* versus *prescriptive* passages. In other words, the Bible doesn't approve of everything it records, and not everything it records is a command for everyone to follow. To learn the difference, we look at who wrote the book, whom they wrote it to, and how the original audience understood it in order to ultimately figure out what the author intended to communicate.

For example, when McLaren takes a broad sweep at how the Bible tells us to behave toward our enemies, he leaves out the fact that God commanded Israel to "utterly destroy" the Canaanites under very special circumstances. Israel was God's chosen people, and they had a unique covenant with him that no one else had. God handed down certain laws and rituals, including various sacrifices offered in the Tabernacle and later the Temple, as well as ceremonial laws, purity laws, dress codes, and dietary laws, that pertained only to them. Also, the *old covenant was understood to be temporary.* It was never meant to be binding on all people through all time. Jeremiah 31 and Ezekiel 36 look forward to a *new covenant* that would replace the old one. So his command to "utterly destroy" the Canaanites was a one-time deal. If there is still any confusion, God made very clear *why* he commanded them to do that. Moses records: "It is because of the wickedness of these nations that the LORD is driving them out before you" (Deuteronomy 9:4). Clearly, this was a specific act of judgment on an evil nation and not a universal command about how to treat our enemies.

We All Must Decide

G. K. Chesterton wrote, "I am incurably convinced that the object of opening the mind, as of opening the mouth, is to shut it again on something solid."[23] After enduring four long months in my discussion group, I knew I needed to make a decision. *Do I just keep my mind hanging open like a garbage bin for endless questions and skeptical attacks—or do I shut it on something solid?* It was time to shut it again—on real answers. I had more than enough questions to research, claims to disprove or verify, and opinions to sort through. And by now, my faith was all but shipwrecked.

The very last class I attended was one in which our spouses were invited, so my husband joined me. The subject: homosexuality. Around this time, there weren't many self-proclaimed evangelicals who affirmed same-sex relationships, but the discussions were beginning to happen all over the country in church classrooms and online community forums. As our discussion ensued, some confessed that they'd had a change of heart.

"It was the Holy Spirit," announced one woman as the reason for her switch from the historic Christian view of sexuality to a more progressive one.

"I made some gay friends," reported another.

At one point, the pastor said, "Well, it's clear to me that the Bible condemns homosexuality . . . so each and every one of you need to decide—how much authority does this book hold in your life?"

Make no mistake . . . this was no question. This was a bold denial of biblical authority. And I was done. It wasn't just because of the pastor's view of homosexuality. It wasn't even because of his view of the Virgin Birth or the historicity of the Old Testament. If we weren't going to rely on the Scriptures to determine our views on everything from salvation to sexuality, we had no common ground.

He was right about something though. In years past, it was assumed that if you called yourself a Christian, you believed in biblical authority. But now as progressive Christianity infiltrates and infects the true church, we all must decide: How much authority does this book hold in our lives? To inform our view of the Bible, we can choose to follow the whims of a godless culture or we can choose to follow Jesus.

I choose Jesus.

10

Hell on Earth?

One of the more interesting things folks will say to me is: "I'm not religious or anything, I just hope that being a good person is enough." To which I always want to say . . . "enough for what?" . . . avoiding the punishment of burning in the eternal fires of some kind of imaginary hell?

Nadia Bolz-Weber

"Everyone in this class is at least seven years old. Did you know that *seven* is the age of accountability? That means that if by seven years old you haven't received Jesus as your personal Lord and Savior, you will be on fire in hell forever while worms slowly eat your flesh for all eternity."

I wish that was the only thing my second-grade teacher ever said about hell. But no. Not only did she remind us of this often, but in Bible class at our Christian elementary school she drilled down. She sat on a stool in front of cardboard ABCs and a cartoon caterpillar calendar with her hands serenely folded in her lap. In a calm but rigid voice, she plumbed the bottomless pit of hell and didn't hold back. Speaking slowly with ominous foreboding, she asked us to close our eyes and imagine the worms . . . imagine the slow and painful torture that awaited anyone who failed to ask Jesus into their heart. Imagine the horror of begging for the sweet release of death that would never come to stop to the torment. *This is forever, kids, and forever never ends. Ever. Did I mention forever?*

That year, my days consisted of learning about math and language, and thinking about eternal conscious torment. My afternoons included chasing Olympic dreams at my local gymnastics center. And my evenings were spent doing everything I could to avoid homework—and panic attacks.

Around this same time, I began to learn about the Rapture. This was supposed to be "good news," but for an eight-year-old already living in almost constant existential crisis, the idea of Jesus unexpectedly beaming his followers up to heaven sounded just about as terrifying as the hordes of insatiable zombie worms that were waiting to feast on my face. Oh, and heaven was forever, too. After someone compared heaven with "an eternal worship service," I couldn't figure out which sounded worse . . . eternal fire or an eternal sing-along.

I began to realize that my main fear wasn't simply the concepts of heaven or hell. *It was eternity.* I was absolutely petrified of living forever . . . no matter where I ended up. Trying to wrap my prepubescent mind around a timeline that never ends—or even worse, God's timeline *never having a beginning*—was too much for my yet-to-be developed frontal lobe to process.

As the years went on, this fear and panic became my new

normal. Laying my head on my pillow at night, I would come up with creative scenarios to distract myself from thinking about hell and eternity. As a creative kid with a wild imagination, I learned from a very young age to use that resourcefulness to escape the haunting contemplations my mind often imposed upon my consciousness. Some nights I was an Olympic gold medal–winning gymnast who ran around the arena smiling and waving before jumping into the arms of my firm but kind and fatherly coach. (Cut me a break. It was the eighties and Mary Lou Retton was adorable.) Other nights I was someone interesting and offbeat, like Punky Brewster or the plucky, yet-to-be-discovered future member of the A-Team.

No matter which fantasy I employed, sometimes it wasn't enough to stave off the impending panic. Thoughts of eternity would slowly materialize like an electric current shooting from the bottom of my feet out the top of my head. Accompanied by instant sweat, rapid heart rate, and chills that flooded every pore, I would squeeze my eyes shut and jump out of bed with an adrenaline rush that could wake the dead. Pacing the room and shaking my hands, I would beg God to please, please make it stop. Eventually it would, but the dread of wondering when it would happen again never did.

Snatching a Friend from the Pit of Hell

As a child, I would occasionally be allowed to attend "big church" with my mom and dad. There was something warm and heavy about big church. Something reverent.

Seriousness and sobriety filled the air, but it wasn't dry or unfeeling. It was electric yet constrained. Alive. I felt something in that place I didn't feel when I was in Sunday school class or youth group. I associated that feeling with the presence of God.

So it was with great hope that, at nineteen, I entered the same sanctuary I had hundreds of times before—but this time with a singular purpose—to save my friend from hell. After graduating from high school, I had taken a hostess job at Chili's and befriended Christina, a food server I worked particularly well with. "You can double-seat me," she would say. "In fact, just feel free to fill up my tables as fast as you can." With the manager breathing down my neck to seat all the tables as *quickly as possible*, most of the servers shooting nasty looks if I filled their sections *too quickly*, and hungry customers griping that they weren't being seated *quickly enough*, my job was a stressful balancing act.

Christina was a party girl, but she was different from my other coworkers. She never tried to shock me with stories of her wild life, nor did she clam up and presume that if she cussed in my presence, she would melt the poor puritanical Christian girl like the green witch in *The Wizard of Oz*.

When I learned that my church was hosting a production of a traveling Christian drama on heaven and hell that toured all over the world, I saw a chance to help my friend meet Jesus. I'd heard stories of people being so moved by the production that the altars were flooded after it was over. This was it. This was the perfect opportunity to share the gospel with Christina. Surely she wouldn't be able to resist the persuasive depictions of heaven and hell. Surely she would realize how quickly this life is over and how important her life-and-death choices would be now. Surely she would give her heart to Christ.

On the day of the performance, Christina met me in the lobby, and we found our seats. Excitement and anticipation hung in the air as the lights faded to black. Under a red-toned hue, Sandi Patty's "Via Dolorosa" was sung as Jesus staggered down the middle aisle carrying his cross. Tears misted my eyes as I watched the depiction of my Savior stumbling to his death—the Savior who meant more to me than heaven or hell. Surely he had it all figured out and I would one day realize that my anxiety had been unnecessary. I snapped to attention as the music suddenly changed to a frantic, drum-driven beat. Regular people just like me began hitting Jesus, whipping him, mocking him, and spitting on him. My breath caught in my throat as I imagined the significance of this. I—a sinner—nailed Jesus to the cross. It was *my* rebellion that put him there, and his great love and mercy that ordained it to happen.

Enter the villain. With a maniacal howling cackle, the devil emerged from his fiery pit to join the abusers in beating Jesus and nailing him to the cross. The devil's face was covered in black-and-white makeup, making him look more like a member of the band KISS than the prince of the power of the air. Thus was my conception of hell and the devil: a raving-mad Gene Simmons look-alike emerging from a red-lit block of dry ice with an evil laugh that rivaled that of Jack Nicholson's Joker.

After Jesus was crucified, he rose again, giving the devil and his gang of demons quite the butt-kicking across the stage before ascending into heaven, where everything was made of white fabric and aluminum foil and everyone wore baggy, floor-length white robes and just kind of stood there for all eternity. For the remainder of the play, we watched person after person find themselves at the shiny tin gates after their untimely deaths. I was on the edge of my seat awaiting the fate of each eternal soul. Would Jesus appear, give them a big hug, and usher them behind the mysterious big white curtain? Or would the devil emerge laughing from his scarlet pit and drag them to hell like something from an Ozzy Osbourne video? Either way, the devil seemed to be having a ball in hell.

I don't remember exactly how the altar call went. Maybe the pastor said something like "With every head bowed and every eye closed, I want to ask if you know where you're going if you die tonight." There was an intense energy in the air as the altar was practically overrun. At one point, the pastor asked us to pray for those who we knew had not made Jesus Lord of their life. Then we were prompted to ask the person next to us, "Would you like me to walk down to the altar with you?" It took all the brass I had to whisper the question to Christina. I imagined she was deeply moved and simply needed a little nudge from a loving friend. I slightly opened my eyes, expecting to see tears rolling down her face. Instead, she was quiet and peaceful, respectfully keeping her eyes closed and her head bowed. "Oh, no thanks," she politely whispered back.

How can this be? Did she miss the part about burning in hell forever? Did she not believe the devil when he announced that he had inspired all the beer commercials on TV? Did she not think that spending eternity in a white-draped, metallic room being hugged by Jesus sounded great? Apparently, she didn't. We left quietly as Christina thanked me for inviting her.

I couldn't figure out why Christina was so unmoved while so many others were captivated and persuaded. I'm sure there are many Christians today who once walked the aisle at a showing of a similar church production. I'm sure they went on to develop a more nuanced theology of heaven and hell. But for many years of my life, my picture of hell mirrored that of this drama.

Love Wins

Even though my understanding of hell wasn't exactly fleshed out, most progressives have a different view of hell altogether. In his book *Love Wins*, Rob Bell suggests that perhaps, rather than being a physical place, hell is simply the literal experience of evil on earth.[1] In other words, hell is the wounds left behind by genocide, rape, and murder. Ironically, this progressive idea of hell is partially true. Every time we turn from the truth of God, we introduce hell into the world. Every time we call evil "good" and good "evil," we create little pockets of hell on earth. But that's not the whole story. The Bible teaches that hell is also an actual place.

The denial of a literal place called hell is now common among progressive Christians, but back in 2011, it was incredibly controversial. Rob Bell incited a firestorm (pun intended) with *Love Wins*. In the introduction, Bell writes,

> A staggering number of people have been taught that a select few Christians will spend forever in a peaceful, joyous place called heaven, while the rest of humanity spends forever in torment and punishment in hell with no chance for anything better. It's been clearly communicated to many that this belief is a central truth of the Christian faith and to reject it is, in essence, to reject Jesus. This is misguided and toxic and ultimately subverts the contagious spread of Jesus's message of love, peace, forgiveness, and joy that our world desperately needs to hear.[2]

Like Bell, Brian Zahnd claims that hell is at odds with Jesus' teaching. He writes,

> Jesus certainly did not lay the foundation for an afterlife theology that claims all non-Christians go to hell. This has become a common way of thinking about heaven and hell—"Christians go to heaven; non-Christians go to hell"—but it is not based on anything Jesus ever said![3]

Franciscan friar and author Richard Rohr goes even further to describe the view of God as a being who inflicts punishment and doles out rewards as unhealthy, "cheap," and "toxic." He writes,

Jesus tells us to love our enemies, but this "cultural"
god sure doesn't. Jesus tells us to forgive "seventy
times seven" times, but this god doesn't. Instead,
this god burns people for all eternity. . . . Most
humans are more loving and forgiving than such
a god. We've developed an unworkable and toxic
image of God that a healthy person would never
trust. . . . Why would you want to spend even an
hour in silence, solitude, or intimacy with such
a god?[4]

So is Richard Rohr correct in saying that a view of God
that includes punishment and reward is evidence of a toxic
mind in need of deep healing? Or is this nothing more than
a manipulative trick—a type of spiritual gaslighting—meant
to make one question their mental health if they disagree
with him?

His view certainly helps explain the appeal of universalism to those who reject the idea that a loving God would
reject those who reject him.

Universalism: The Way We Would Do It

Many modern Christians have some serious misconceptions about hell and the afterlife. Some of our views of hell
have been shaped by Dante's *Inferno* of the Middle Ages,
others by the fire-and-brimstone preachers of the first Great
Awakening, and still others by a vexing second grade teacher
or a traveling church drama. So it's not difficult to understand

why universalism has become such an attractive alternative for so many Christians who struggle to reconcile the goodness of God with his supposed "torture chamber."

There are several different understandings of universalism, but put most simply, it's the belief that all human beings (and in some cases, even fallen angels) will be saved and spend eternity with God. Some in the progressive Christian paradigm deny the idea that sin separates us from God altogether, rendering any need for a meaningful "salvation" unnecessary. A view that adopts more Christian language is called universal reconciliation, which holds that while Jesus is the only way to salvation, all humans will eventually be reconciled to God through Jesus. William Paul Young holds this belief and calls it universal salvation,[5] and Nadia Bolz-Weber calls it Christo-centric universalism: "I confess that I am a Christo-centric universalist. What that means to me is that, whatever God was accomplishing, especially on the cross, that Christological event, was for the restoration and redemption and reconciliation of all things and all people and all Creation—everyone."[6]

Universalism was first suggested by church father Origen (possibly echoing Clement of Alexandria) in the third century, although there is much scholarly debate on exactly *what* he believed about universalism and how ardently he defended it. There is even debate about *when*, precisely, his teachings were deemed heretical. I'll leave those debates to the scholars. But in his two-volume history and interpretation of universalism, *The Devil's Redemption*, scholar Michael McClymond traces the doctrine from Origen in the early third century to influential theologian Karl Barth in the mid-twentieth century to today. Dubbing it "the opiate of the theologians," he notes how universalism has gained momentum in the last five hundred years and "fits the age we inhabit." He points out, "It's the way we would want the world to be. Some imagine that a more loving and less judgmental church would be better positioned to win new adherents. Yet perfect love appeared in history—and he was crucified."[7]

It's not difficult to understand why universalism is so appealing. No one wants to imagine their unbelieving friends, neighbors, and family members spending eternity in torment. It's an easy fix to a troubling idea. But as much as it may bring comfort, I learned that it is not biblical, nor does it represent the historic witness of the church.

In his international, peer-reviewed theological journal article about the history of universalism, New Testament scholar Dr. Richard Bauckham noted,

> Until the nineteenth century almost all Christian theologians taught the reality of eternal torment in hell. Here and there, outside the theological mainstream, were some who believed that the wicked would be finally annihilated.... Even fewer were the advocates of universal salvation, though these few included some major theologians of the early church. Eternal punishment was firmly asserted in official creeds and confessions of the churches. It must have seemed as indispensable a part of universal Christian belief as the doctrines of the Trinity and the incarnation.[8]

Although universalism appeals to our modern sensibilities, it is not what the Bible teaches. As we discussed in the last chapter, God's wrath for sin ensures that his followers will not spend eternity coexisting with sin. Through the sacrificial death of Jesus, we are invited into an eternal Kingdom that will vanquish sin and death forever.

Where in the World Is Hell?

A few years before *Love Wins* was released, I had been forced to grapple with my own simplistic beliefs regarding the afterlife. I learned that when the progressive pastor told me that, yes, he believed in the existence of hell, he had redefined that word too. He revealed in a later class that he believed hell was some kind of rehabilitation program, or possibly the consequences of our wrong actions that we experience here on earth. In keeping with the hopeful agnosticism he claimed in the beginning, he wasn't sure, but he was hopeful that hell wasn't what Christians had historically believed.

Given my simplistic and incorrect assumption that hell was a torture chamber and heaven was an eternal bore—you would think I would be all over that like jelly on peanut butter. So why wasn't I? Why did it bother me to think that hell wasn't real? Was it because I secretly relished the thought of unbelievers being tormented forever? Certainly not! In fact, I had experienced panic attacks over that very idea. Was it because the doctrine of hell was so deeply ingrained in my psyche that it gave some kind of "sick coherence to my world,"[9] as Richard Rohr claims? Is Rohr right that I need "deep healing" because I believe in concepts like reward and punishment?[10]

As I began to take a serious look at the historic and biblical view of hell, I learned that the biblical view of hell is a little more mysterious than I thought. There is a lot the Bible doesn't reveal, but it does tell us that hell isn't something included in the original creation that God called "good." When God created the heavens and the earth in Genesis 1, hell was not a part of that. Like rust would not exist without metal, hell would not exist if it were not for Satan's choice to rebel (see Matthew 25:41). In this way, Satan was the one who effectively unleashed hell on earth.

In the New Testament, hell is described as

- a fiery lake of burning sulfur (Revelation 21:8);
- everlasting destruction (2 Thessalonians 1:9);
- banishment from the presence of the Lord and the glory of his might (2 Thessalonians 1:9);
- the punishment of eternal fire (Jude 1:7);
- a lake of fire (Revelation 20:13-15); and
- the wine of God's wrath; torment with fire and sulfur in the presence of the holy angels and in the presence of the Lamb (Revelation 14:9-10).

Jesus himself described hell as

- eternal punishment (Matthew 25:46);
- a blazing furnace where "there will be weeping and gnashing of teeth" (Matthew 13:50);

- a place where the fire never goes out (Mark 9:43);
- a place where "their worm does not die and the fire is not quenched" (Mark 9:48, where Jesus is quoting Isaiah 66:24); and
- outer darkness; that place where "there will be weeping and gnashing of teeth" (Matthew 8:12; 22:13; 25:30).

Notice how Jesus uses three different types of imagery to describe hell—fire *and* darkness *and* worms that don't die. For fire and darkness to coexist, one would have to be taken as a metaphor. Literal fire would light the darkness, so literal darkness would not be possible in the presence of fire. This, along with the fact that hell was originally created for the devil and his demons (who are spirit beings and don't have physical bodies to be affected by literal flames), has led many theologians to conclude that these three images—fire, darkness, and worms—are metaphors.

Dr. Norm Geisler and Dr. Thomas Howe write,

Both "fire" and "darkness" are powerful figures of speech which appropriately describe the unthinkable reality of hell. It is like fire because it is a place of destruction and torment. Yet, it is like outer darkness because people are lost there forever. While hell is a literal place, not every description of it should be taken literally. Some powerful figures of speech are used to portray this literal place. Its horrible reality, wherein body and soul will suffer forever, goes far beyond any mere figure of speech that may be used to describe it.[11]

But even if those terms are metaphors, that shouldn't bring us any relief. It just means there aren't words to describe how awful a place hell is. Theologian J. I. Packer describes hell this way: "Hell is . . . the negation of fellowship with the Lord. It's the negation of pleasure. It's the negation of any form of contentment."[12]

Imagine an existence completely devoid of anything good. Without any passing feeling of peace or joy. No beauty. No hope. No love. Nothing to look forward to. Utter despair. Forever trapped within the torment of a bad dream. It's difficult for us to imagine such a state because all of us, from the most hardened atheist to the most ardently devoted Christian, have *no idea* what life would be like outside of the presence of God's goodness and love. We all experience God's presence in the world. This is what theologians refer to as "common grace," and we don't even have a category for what it would be like to be conscious apart from that reality. This is what J. I. Packer refers to as the "heart" of the doctrine of hell. It's life apart from the love and goodness of God and under the complete control and domination of sin. Packer remarked, "It's difficult to talk about hell because it is more awful than we have words for."[13]

As difficult as the subject is, it is often repeated that Jesus talked about hell more than anyone. He often used the word *Gehenna* to describe hell, which was a reference to the Valley of Hinnom, where ancient pagans and Israelites sacrificed their children by fire to the god Molech. God turned this cursed place, where sin and evil were unrestrained, into a place of judgment, calling it "the Valley of Slaughter" (Jeremiah 19:6).

Recent scholarship points out that the Jews of Jesus' time and place understood hell to be a place of punishment after judgment. There are examples in first-century Jewish writings in which the "furnace of Gehenna" is depicted as a pit of torment that comes after final judgement.[14] In other words, it didn't *simply* refer to a valley where their ancestors did horrible things. Gehenna was understood to be hell. Jesus knew this, and if he wanted to talk about Gehenna in a different way than was commonly understood, he would have had to go out of his way to make that point. But he didn't. He used the word *Gehenna* interchangeably with hell.

Jesus often taught theology by telling parables. One of those parables is found in Matthew 25, where he describes the Kingdom of Heaven being like ten virgins waiting for their bridegroom. Five are wise and five are foolish. The five wise virgins brought oil for their lamps, while the five foolish ones brought none. When the bridegroom arrives, the foolish virgins are out of oil. While they go to the dealers to buy more, the door to the wedding feast is shut. And once it is shut, it does not open again. So here we have Jesus—all-inclusive, tolerant, and never-judgy Jesus—shutting the door to his Kingdom. After this, he tells another parable in which he once again describes separating true followers from false ones—the false ones being cast into outer darkness. After these two parables, he teaches about the final judgment. Sheep and Goats. The sheep find eternal life while the goats are condemned to "eternal punishment" (verse 46).

These words were some of the final recorded teachings of Jesus before his arrest and crucifixion. He wanted his followers to know that there would be a final judgment. There would be eternal life and eternal punishment. The door to his Kingdom would one day close. He urges us to be ready. Despite the progressive Christian attempt to soften or reinterpret these teachings, I couldn't shake the power of Jesus' words.

And as I continued my research, I discovered that the earliest Christian sources agree with the New Testament. The *nature* of hell is debated, but three things are made clear. First, hell is eternal. Second, in hell souls are conscious. Third, hell is torment.

As I thought through the nature and justice of hell, I realized that I had been operating under some serious misconceptions about what hell is and why it exists. My guess is that many Christians, and a great many atheists and agnostics, also misunderstand what hell is all about.

Correcting Misconception #1: People in Hell Are Repentant

When I was a little girl, I imagined that the poor souls "gnashing their teeth" in hell were unlucky victims who simply never got the chance to respond to God's love. Like the beer-drinking teenagers whose car was run over by a train in the church play (yes, that was actually one of the scenes), the gnashing of teeth was the physical manifestation of their tearful grief and repentant sorrow over never having had the chance to give their lives to Christ. If only someone had shared the gospel before it was too late! But the Bible gives us a different picture.

Gnashing of teeth is written about several times in Scripture. In the Old Testament, it typically refers to something enemies do in rage and defiance of their foe. Lamentations 2:16 describes the enemies of Jerusalem taunting her by hissing and gnashing their teeth in joyful celebration of her demise. Psalm 37:12 depicts the wicked gnashing their teeth at the righteous as they plot against them. In Psalm 35:16, David characterizes those who gnash their teeth at him as "profane mockers" who rejoice when he stumbles. Even Job uses the imagery of the gnashing of teeth to describe God's wrath (Job 16:9). In the New Testament, Acts 7 gives us the last moments of Stephen's life, just before he goes down in history as the first martyr of the Christian faith. As members of the Sanhedrin pick up stones to execute him, they become filled with rage and "gnashed their teeth" (verse 54, NIV) at him.

This is hardly the picture of an innocent soul weeping in repentant remorse. It's a snapshot of the active anger of an enemy. It's the opposite of repentance and godly sorrow. Perhaps this is why C. S. Lewis famously wrote that "the gates of hell are locked on the inside."[15] I don't know if he's right, but it certainly seems an apt description of the ongoing rebellion of those who are kept out of God's Kingdom.

In this way, hell is not some kind of divine torture chamber in which God sadistically enjoys the torment of those who reject him. It's God giving them their way. Hell is a place for those who reject God. And God will not force anyone into his Kingdom who doesn't want to be under his rule. And he can't let sin and corruption in the door, even for those who want the benefits of heaven but don't want to turn from their sin to follow him.

Correcting Misconception #2: The Devil Is in Charge of Hell

As in the church play that depicted Satan emerging from his eternal fire party to claim those souls who belonged to him, I somehow imagined that the devil was having fun in hell. With a red throne, a pitchfork, demonic servants, and endless supplies of human souls to torture, I pictured a devil who was quite happy to be king of the underworld in his inferno of misery. Have you noticed that just about every popular reference to the devil and hell in movies and television depicts him this way? From late-nineties Al Pacino in *The Devil's Advocate* to Adam Sandler in the 2000 movie *Little Nicky* to more current titles like the television show *Lucifer*, the message is clear: The devil is sexy, smart, and the mayor of his hometown.

But this is far from the biblical picture of hell. When Jesus describes the final judgment in Matthew 25, he says he will separate people like a shepherd separates sheep from goats. When he depicts what will happen to the goats, he says they will depart from him into "the eternal fire prepared for the devil and his angels" (verse 41). So it's clear that hell was not created for people. It was created as a type of quarantine for evil—namely, the devil and demons.

Revelation 20:7-10 tells us that Jesus finally deals with Satan for good: "The devil who had deceived them was thrown into the lake of fire and sulfur where the beast and the false prophet were, and they will be tormented day and night forever and ever." In other words, the devil and his demons will not be ruling or tormenting anyone or having fun. They themselves will be tormented forever in this place God created just for them—hell.

Correcting Misconception #3: Everyone Gets the Same Punishment

When I was a child, I had a babysitter who was a nasty woman. Not in the pop-culture way of defining female empowerment, but in the mean-spirited, harsh, critical, cold-hearted way in which the word is typically used to describe an unpleasant person. She was not nice. She once scolded me for acting like a baby because I wet my pants while searching in vain for a bathroom in an unfamiliar house. She claimed to be a Christian.

I once read an article about a man who sold all his earthly possessions to take care of the homeless. Every day, he would walk into the streets, find the most destitute of human beings, bring them back to his small apartment, bathe them, feed them, and offer them shelter. His entire life was devoted to helping others. He was humble and kind. He was a Buddhist.

So how was I to make sense of the fact that, according to my beliefs, the nasty Christian was going to heaven while the benevolent Buddhist was going to hell? This was hard to figure out because, although I understood the concept of grace with my mind, my heart hadn't gotten the message. Grace isn't about being rewarded for doing and saying the right things. It's not about getting what you deserve. It's about *not* getting what you deserve. Grace is Jesus looking at every human and saying, "You deserve death because of sin, but I'll take what you deserve and offer you the eternal life that I deserve."

When I looked at the Buddhist and the babysitter through the lens of grace, I understood that being a part of God's Kingdom is not about earning our way in. It's not about who gives away the most money or feeds the most homeless people or who's the nicest. In the case of the Buddhist, it's hardwired into his belief system to work off bad karma and enter Nirvana. But the prophet Isaiah tells us that we are so infected by sin that the good we do is like filthy rags (64:6, NIV). Romans 3:20 tells us, "No one will be declared righteous in God's sight by the works of the law" (NIV). It goes on to explain that the purpose of the law is to make us aware of our sin. We are all sick with sin, and Jesus is the only cure.

So what about the kindhearted Buddhist who bathed and fed the homeless? If he dies before he puts his faith in Christ, will he get the same punishment as Hitler while the nasty babysitter enjoys eternal bliss (assuming she was truly a Christian)? I don't think so. And here's why.

In the Old Testament, different sins incur different punishments. Some of those punishments are more severe than others. The greater the sin, the greater the punishment. Jesus echoes this idea at his trial and sentencing in

John 19:11-12, where he tells Pilate, "The one who handed me over to you is guilty of a greater sin" (NIV). In Luke 12:42-48, Jesus tells a parable about different servants receiving differing degrees of punishment based on what they knew about the master's will. He concludes by saying "that servant who knew his master's will but did not get ready or act according to his will, will receive a severe beating. But the one who did not know, and did what deserved a beating, will receive a light beating. Everyone to whom much was given, of him much will be required" (verses 47-48).

In a shocking pronouncement of "woe" in Matthew 11, Jesus condemns two whole cities to a harsher judgment in the afterlife than Sodom. (Tell that to anyone who claims that Jesus was a tolerant and all-inclusive guru.) The Bible regularly speaks of sin and judgment with varying levels of severity and punishment. Learning and understanding this helped me make sense of what I read about the justice of God in the Bible. God is not unjust or simplistic in his judgments. He is perfectly holy and will deal with sin appropriately.

And as I was reminded by theologian Clay Jones in his book *Why Does God Allow Evil? Compelling Answers for Life's Toughest Questions*, I, like many people, tend to gloss over the fallenness of humanity. I think of people who do good things as good people . . . those who bake cookies, play with children, and help their friends in need. But Jones points out that some of the greatest atrocities perpetuated by humans, including genocide, were mostly committed by normal people like you and me.

Even the Nazis had sweet grandmas who baked cookies for the youth rallies.

"Will Only a Few Be Saved?"

One of my fellow students raised this question in class one day. Is the idea that only a select few people will enter the Kingdom of Heaven realistic? Is it fair? Is it plausible? Interestingly, this is a question Jesus' disciples asked him directly. We don't have to wonder about the answer. Jesus responded, "Strive to enter through the narrow door. For many, I tell you, will seek to enter and will not be able" (Luke 13:24). He goes on to describe the master of the house shutting and locking the door. Those who are outside will not come in.

Why, then, does Revelation 21:25 say that the gates of heaven will "never be shut by day"? Is this God's way of saying, "The door is always open . . . it's never too late"? As I reasoned through this, I read a bit further in that same chapter. The text lets us know that this great city has very high and sturdy walls. By nature, walls are constructed to exclude people who don't belong inside. Who doesn't belong inside? Verse 27 gives us the answer: "Nothing unclean will ever enter it, nor anyone who does what is detestable or false, but only those who are written in the Lamb's book of life." In the ancient world, cities shut their gates as a security measure. But those measures won't be necessary in the new heaven and new earth. There is no need to shut the gates because sin will have already been contained and dealt with. No one will be leaving hell to enter heaven.

In the end, I've come to see that hell is not only necessary, it is ultimately loving and just. If someone desires sin and corruption now, what would make me think he would desire to be separated from sin and corruption for eternity? If someone continually chooses to hate God and reject his gift of reconciliation in this life, what would make me think she will desire to be in his Kingdom forever in the next? And here's something to ponder: If someone wants to bring their self-serving sin into heaven, what would it say about God if he allowed it in?

I'm about to say something unpopular. We live in a culture in which it is considered arrogant and even hateful to make dogmatic claims about reality. But if we believe the Bible is true—if we follow our Lord Jesus—we must affirm this alongside him: Heaven is real. Hell is real. And one day, the door will close.

11

Cosmic Child Abuse?

That God needed to be appeased with blood is not beautiful. It's horrific.

Michael Gungor, 2017

I, Alisa Childers, am a sinner. I would call myself the *worst* of sinners if the title wasn't already taken by the apostle Paul (see 1 Timothy 1:15). I know how deeply I've rebelled against God. I know how desperately I need a Savior.

This is why the Cross is so precious to me. This is why an attack on the Cross is an attack on the very core of what it means to be a Christian. As we'll see, an attack on the Cross is an attack on the nature of God himself.

Did Jesus Need to Die?

"The religious view of the people of ancient Mesopotamia was that the gods were angry and that the only way to appease them was with blood," the progressive pastor articulated during a sermon one Sunday morning. In an uncharacteristic flourish, he extended his arms as he mimicked an ancient Jew trying to wrangle a bull and drag it to the Tent of Meeting. "That's why the Israelites *thought* they needed to drag goats and bulls to the altar and make sacrifices to Yahweh," he said. "But when Jesus came along and said that he fulfilled the law, he was telling them they didn't have to do that. They never did." Then he released his hands and lifted them slightly to indicate the relief and freedom of the ended struggle. "Jesus did not come to abolish the law." After a climactic pause, he spoke very slowly: "He . . . came . . . to . . . end . . . it."

Many questions swirled in my head as I looked around to see if anyone else was as shocked as I was. Nope. Just me. Most of the congregation seemed to be utterly caught up in his passionate discourse.

Did he really just say that the Israelites only thought *they had to make sacrifices?*

Is he arguing that the entire Old Testament sacrificial system was just well-intentioned mimicry of the surrounding culture?

Is he implying that Moses got it wrong?

Wait a minute. We understand Jesus' death through the lens of the sacrificial system. If it wasn't something God instituted, why did Jesus even need to die?

This was the key question, and a few days later I was able to ask the pastor about it. He responded thoughtfully, "Well, I think Jesus *did* need to die. He needed to die because of his love for us. He knew that people were bloodthirsty and violent, so he laid his life down and gave us our pound of flesh. It was the ultimate act of love."

He stripped the Cross of the Atonement and shrouded it in a cloak of "love." At the time, this seemed shocking. I couldn't imagine that a Christian would see Jesus' atoning sacrifice as anything but beautiful. As time went by, I began to notice more progressive Christians speaking out against something they understood to be "cosmic child abuse."

Redeeming Love or Cosmic Child Abuse?

As I began to study the atonement, I noticed that the Bible uses various metaphors and descriptive language to illustrate what Jesus' death on the cross accomplished. As an avid Bible reader from my youth, none of this was new, but until now, I didn't realize that people tended to pick one metaphor over another. For me, they had all functioned like different facets on the same beautiful diamond. For example, Mark 10:45 describes Christ as our "ransom." First Corinthians 15:54-57 tells us that Jesus defeated the powers of sin and death, giving us victory. Philippians 3:10-12 presents Jesus as a moral example to follow, inviting the Christian to become "like him in his death." Galatians 4:4-7 explains that Jesus redeemed us from the law so that we could be received by God as adopted sons and daughters.

One biblical description in particular, that "Christ died for our sins," is a core essential of the historic Christian faith. This tenet is mentioned in the early creed, which Paul recorded in 1 Corinthians 15:3-5 and we discussed in chapter 3. Eventually this doctrine came to be known as substitutionary atonement. It means that Jesus died in our place . . . as our substitute. But the Bible tells us that Jesus also paid the penalty for our sin, which adds a deeper element to our understanding. This is called penal substitutionary atonement. The word *penal* has to do with punishment and penalty. Of all the biblical descriptions of atonement, this is the one most commonly rejected by progressive Christians. Progressive author Tony Jones calls this the "payment model," which he roundly rejects.[1] It can be summed up this way:

- We humans are fallen creatures and sinners by nature. (Romans 3:23; 5:12; Ephesians 2:1-3)
- Our sin separates us from God. (Isaiah 59:2; Ephesians 2:12; 4:18)
- The consequence for our sin is death. (Genesis 2:17; Ezekiel 18:20; Romans 5:12; 6:23)
- Jesus, God incarnate, died for our sins in our place, as our substitute. (Isaiah 53; Romans 3:21-25; 5:8-10; Acts 20:28; 1 Corinthians 15:3; 2 Corinthians 5:21; Galatians 1:3-4; Ephesians 5:1-2; Hebrews 9:26; 1 Timothy 2:5-6; 1 Peter 3:18)
- Jesus paid the price for our sins. (1 Corinthians 6:20; 7:23; Galatians 3:13; 1 Peter 1:18-19; 2:24; 3:18)

- His sacrifice satisfied the wrath of God (John 3:36, Romans 3:24-25; 5:9; Hebrews 2:17; 1 John 2:2; 4:10) so we could be reconciled to God. (Romans 5:10-11; 2 Corinthians 5:18-21; Colossians 1:20; Ephesians 2:16)

This belief has united Christians throughout the ages and across cultures and continents. It's the story Scripture tells from the fall of Eden in Genesis to its restoration in Revelation. In Genesis 3:21, God hints at the necessity for sacrifice when he kills an animal and uses its skins to cover Adam and Eve's nakedness. In Revelation, Jesus is called the Lamb several times. Angels and elders even sing to Jesus: "With your blood you *purchased* for God persons from every tribe and language and people and nation" (Revelation 5:9, NIV, emphasis mine). Verse 12 continues, "Worthy is the Lamb, who was slain." Calling Jesus "the Lamb" is a reference back to the Old Testament sacrificial system.

For example, Leviticus 4 and 5 tell us about two of the sacrifices the Old Testament Jews were required to bring before the Lord—sin offerings and guilt offerings. Together, these offerings focused on making atonement for the sin of the offeror. These sacrifices would require a bull (for the high priest or congregation) or a flock animal (for regular citizens) to be slaughtered, with some of its blood placed on the horns of the altar and the rest poured out at the base of the altar. Leviticus 4:32 specifically mentions bringing a lamb for a sin offering. In the New Testament, John the Baptist explicitly identifies Jesus with this practice by declaring, "Behold, the

Lamb of God, who takes away the sin of the world!" (John 1:29). In 1 Corinthians 5:7, the apostle Paul calls Jesus "our Passover lamb" who "has been sacrificed." This is a direct comparison with the slaughtered lambs whose blood the Israelites placed on their doorposts during the final plague in Egypt. This blood is what saved their firstborn children from death. In other words, the lamb died so their children didn't have to.

Despite the abundance of biblical testimony, the one thing that virtually all progressive Christian thought leaders agree on is that Jesus didn't die to pay the penalty for our sin. He was crucified by an angry mob for speaking truth to power, and his love and forgiveness toward those who killed him is the example we all should follow. According to progressive Christians, Jesus didn't need to die, but he submitted himself to the will of the people. According to their wisdom, the historic view makes God nothing more than an abusive father.

Although the idea of "cosmic child abuse" has been around for quite a while in more theologically liberal circles, it crept into the evangelical mainstream through the wildly popular book *The Shack*. Released in 2007, *The Shack* has sold over twenty million copies (ten million copies were in print by 2010) and spent 136 weeks on the *New York Times* Best Sellers List.[2] The book features Mack, a father of five whose daughter Missy was kidnapped and murdered by a serial killer. While grieving, he finds a note in his mailbox from "Papa," inviting him to meet at the shack where it is believed Missy was killed. Once there, Mack meets the members of the Trinity, each taking the form of a different character. Papa, the Father, is an African-American woman. Jesus is a Middle Eastern carpenter. The Holy Spirit is an Asian woman named Sarayu. During his time at the shack, Mack has many theological conversations with these characters about evil, suffering, atonement, and the nature of God.

Because it was written in novel form, some Christians have had difficulty discerning the theology behind the book. I've met many people who admit they had "red flags" about some of what they read but ultimately dismissed those concerns because they were so deeply moved by the book's emotional story line. In one scene, Mack asks Papa why Jesus had to die. Although the reason is left a bit unclear, Papa tells him that Jesus' death reconciled her (the Father) to the whole world. When Mack asks if she is only reconciled to those who believe in Jesus, Papa responds, "The whole world, Mack."[3] Though not an outright affirmation of universalism, scenes like this left many Christians scratching their heads about what the book was actually communicating.

A few years after *The Shack* came out, its author, William Paul Young, released a theological treatise called *Lies We Believe about God*. In it, the hints and implications he made in his novel are articulated with clarity and confidence. Young affirms universal reconciliation and denies the substitutionary atonement of Jesus. He writes,

> Who originated the Cross?
> If God did, then we worship a cosmic abuser, who in Divine Wisdom created a means to torture human beings in the most painful and abhorrent manner. . . .

The alternative is that the Cross originated
with us human beings. This deviant device is the
iconic manifestation of our blind commitment to
darkness....
And how did God respond to this profound
brokenness?
God submitted to it. God climbed willingly onto
our torture device and met us at the deepest and
darkest place of our diabolical imprisonment to our
own lies, and by submitting once and for all, God
destroyed its power....
And how would we religious people interpret
this sacrifice? We would declare that it was God
who killed Jesus, slaughtering Him as a necessary
appeasement for His bloodthirsty need for justice.[4]

He explains why the idea that the Father would have required
the Son to take our punishment is abhorrent to him.

One of the narratives about God is that because
of sin, God required child sacrifice to appease a
sense of righteous indignation and the fury of
holiness—Jesus being the ultimate child sacrifice.
Well, if God is like that, then doesn't it make sense
that we would follow in God's footsteps? But we
know intuitively that such a thought is wrong,
desperately wrong.[5]

Like my former pastor, many progressives suggest that
the sacrificial system wasn't part of God's plan; instead, the

Israelites adopted the practice from other ancient cultures. Progressive British minister Steve Chalke says,

> Penal substitution is tantamount to "child abuse—a vengeful Father punishing his Son for an offence he has not even committed." Though the sheer bluntness of this imagery (not original to me of course) might shock some, in truth, it is only a stark "unmasking" of the violent, pre-Christian thinking behind such a theology.[6]

Rob Bell adds, "God didn't set up the sacrificial system. People did. The sacrificial system evolved as humans developed rituals and rites to help them deal with their guilt and fear."[7] The first Christians, Bell claims, took it one step further when they chose to "interpret Jesus' death through the lens of the sacrificial system, trusting that the peace humans had been longing for with God for thousands of years was in fact a reality."[8]

Brian Zahnd, the author of *Sinners in the Hands of a Loving God*, writes that "Calvary is not where we see how violent God is; Calvary is where we see how violent our civilization is."[9] Zahnd contends that the modern understanding of penal substitution is a doctrine developed by John Calvin, having first appeared in another form in the eleventh century.[10] Many progressives agree, pointing to the Italian monk Anselm, who worked out what is called the satisfaction theory, which is based on the principle that someone who has offended another must make restitution to the one he has wronged according to that person's status. As the King of kings, God required compensation far beyond humanity's ability to pay. Only Jesus—someone fully divine (equal status with God) and fully human (the one who owed the debt)—could offer himself on our behalf. Richard Rohr and other progressives argue that Anselm developed this theory because it closely aligned with the Middle Age feudal understanding and practice of justice.[11]

Not only did the sacrificial system originate with humans, progressives say, but the belief that Christ sacrificed himself on our behalf is dangerous because it distorts our view of the Father. "God didn't need the blood of sacrifices. People did," says Bell. "God didn't need to kill someone to be 'happy' with humanity. What kind of God would that be? Awful. Horrific."[12] Zahnd writes that "the only thing God will call justice is setting the world right, not punishing an innocent substitute for the petty sake of appeasement."[13] Chalke adds that "the simple truth is that if God does not relate to his only Son as a perfect Father, neither can we relate to him as such."[14]

Another problem with this view of atonement, some progressives say, is that when our theology emphasizes Jesus' death, we miss the significance of the example he set for us through his life. Richard Rohr explains: "I believe that Jesus' death on the cross is a revelation of the infinite and participatory love of God, not some bloody payment required by God's offended justice to rectify the problem of sin. Such a story line is way too small and problem-oriented."[15] Elsewhere, he says that "Jesus came to change the mind of humanity about God. . . . There was no transaction necessary, there was not a blood sacrifice necessary."[16] Regarding the atonement views of "modern Christians," Rachel Held Evans writes,

> "Jesus came to die," they often say, referring to a view of Christianity that reduces the gospel to a transaction, whereby God needed a spotless sacrifice to atone for the world's sins and thus sacrificed Jesus on the cross so believers could go to heaven. In this view, Jesus basically shows up to post our bail.[17]

Though many progressives suggest that we focus more on Jesus' life and teaching, they don't deny that Jesus died for us. The reasons they give, however, are very different from those who believe Jesus gave his life as a ransom for humanity. In short, they say, Jesus allowed a bloodthirsty world to kill him to show us how we should love and forgive others. Zahnd explains,

> The cross is not a picture of payment; the cross is a picture of forgiveness. . . . The cross is not where God finds a whipping boy to vent his rage upon; the cross is where God saves the world through self-sacrificing love. . . . The sacrifice of Jesus was necessary to convince us to quit producing sacrificial victims, but it was not necessary to convince God to forgive.[18]

This understanding of why Jesus died naturally affects how many progressives view various church practices—including the Eucharist. Based on this new interpretation, Brian McLaren offers an alternative way to understand Communion:

> In a table-centered eucharistic understanding, atoning or appeasing sacrifices are simply unnecessary. Nothing need be done to appease a hostile God, because through Christ, God has self-revealed as inherently gracious and kind, seeking reconciliation; not hostile and vengeful, needing appeasement.[19]

Wrath of the Straw Man

Almost every one of the quotes above mischaracterizes the historic Christian view of the Cross in some way. For instance, Brian Zahnd says that "Good Friday is not about divine wrath; Good Friday is about divine love."[20] Christians have always seen the Cross as the ultimate picture of divine love, but they also recognize that a righteous God cannot abide sin—not because he's intolerant but because of his goodness and holiness, and because of the havoc sin wreaks on his creation. Old Testament scholar Jay Sklar refers to sin as an "acid that mars and destroys whatever it touches." He notes, "The Lord is not being a killjoy by forbidding sin; he is being a loving Savior."[21]

Notice, too, how progressives describe God and his actions using words like *hostile, torture, petty, abuser, abhorrent,* and *bloodthirsty,* even though these are at odds with how God is described throughout Scripture as Father, Creator, Supplier, Provider, Healer, and Shepherd. Likewise, phrases like *whipping boy* and *child sacrifice* are used to describe Jesus and his fate. All of this rhetorical and manipulative language helps to construct a logical fallacy called a straw man. In critical thinking, a straw man is created when someone misrepresents their opponent's view, building a version that is much easier to refute or knock down, like toppling a scarecrow instead of a real man. In the same way, the type of wrath and justice that is usually rejected by progressives is not the biblical version, but a straw man based on the type of wrath that humans experience rather than the true wrath of God.

What is the first thing that comes to your mind when you hear the word *wrath*? For me it's an image that seamlessly fuses the Ringwraiths from The Lord of the Rings trilogy, Ricardo Montalbán from the old Star Trek movie *The Wrath of Khan*, and a curmudgeonly Southern preacher (maybe dressed up as a Ringwraith?) spitting and shouting from his pulpit high above the heads of his frightened parishioners.

It's understandable that a good many Christians are confused about God's wrath. For some, *wrath* conjures memories of an angry father flying into a drunken rage over almost nothing. For others, it stirs up childhood feelings of fear and dread over the school bully or an abusive teacher. Our human examples of wrath often become our understanding of God's wrath, which is entirely different.

Colossians 3:8 tells us that *unrighteous carnal* wrath is a sin: "Now you must put them all away: anger, wrath, malice, slander, and obscene talk from your mouth." But across the

Old and New Testaments, Scripture gives us a metaphor to help us understand God's wrath.

Not that kind of wrath

All throughout the Old Testament (and later in the New), the Bible compares God's wrath to a cup. The prophet Isaiah wrote that the people of Jerusalem had "drunk from the hand of the LORD the *cup* of his wrath" (Isaiah 51:17, emphasis mine). Jeremiah echoes a similar sentiment: "Thus the LORD, the God of Israel, said to me: 'Take from my hand this *cup* of the wine of wrath, and make all the nations to whom I send you drink it'" (Jeremiah 25:15). Later, in the book of Revelation, we find out that anyone who receives the mark of the beast will "drink the wine of God's wrath, poured full strength into the cup of his anger" (Revelation 14:9-10).

Jesus mentions this cup one more time when he is praying in the garden of Gethsemane the night before he faces the Cross: "My Father, if it be possible, let this cup pass from me; nevertheless, not as I will, but as you will" (Matthew 26:39). With the biblical understanding of the cup, we can better understand Jesus' anguish in the garden. He wasn't just asking about the physical suffering he was about to endure. He was also getting ready to drink the cup of God's wrath—the cup that God had patiently waited to pour out on his Son.

The wrath of God is not a divine temper tantrum triggered by erratic feelings of offense and hatred. The wrath of God is not petty or spiteful. It is the controlled and righteous judgment of anything that opposes the Lord's perfect nature and love. We should be very thankful for the wrath of God. The wrath of God means that there will be justice for the victims of the Holocaust. The wrath of God means that ISIS won't get away with its atrocities. The wrath of God means that one day all evil and sin will be quarantined and that those who have put their trust in Jesus will be entirely separated from wickedness and safe from the clutches of suffering and corruption forever. God's wrath exists *because* he is love.

Croatian theologian Miroslav Volf realized this after witnessing the horrors of the Bosnian war:

> I used to think that wrath was unworthy of God. Isn't God love? Shouldn't divine love be beyond wrath? God is love, and God loves every person and every creature. That's exactly why God is wrathful against some of them. My last resistance to the idea of God's wrath was a casualty of the war in former Yugoslavia, the region from which I come. According to some estimates, 200,000 people were killed and over 3,000,000 were displaced. *My* villages and cities were destroyed, *my* people shelled day in and day out, some of them brutalized beyond imagination, and I could not imagine God not being angry. Or think of Rwanda in the last decade of the past century, where 800,000 people were hacked to death in one hundred days! How did God react to the carnage? By doting on the perpetrators in a grandparently fashion? By refusing to condemn the bloodbath but instead

affirming the perpetrators' basic goodness? Wasn't God fiercely angry with them? Though I used to complain about the indecency of the idea of God's wrath, I came to think that I would have to rebel against a God who *wasn't* wrathful at the sight of the world's evil. God isn't wrathful in spite of being love. God is wrathful *because* God is love.[22]

A robust theology of the Cross is what will withstand the storms, sufferings, persecutions, and hardships that Jesus promised would confront those who are his true followers. That is a hard promise—not the kind you'll find in a superficial pocket promise book. But along with his promise, Jesus left us this magnificent assurance: "Be of good cheer; I have overcome the world" (John 16:33, KJV).

Son of a Bit

A mother I know has a young son with a developmental delay called receptive language disorder. Basically, this just means that he has a hard time understanding what people are saying to him. From an early age, he would not answer questions but simply repeat what was asked. If she asked him, "Do you want a snack?" he would reply, "Want a snack?" It took a long time for him to learn the difference between a question and a statement. Because of his limited language abilities, he would often struggle with anger and frustration.

One day when he asked to watch a certain TV show, she told him no. That's a word he *did* understand. Instantly, he turned fire-engine red, looked right at her, and roared, "*You are such a bit!*" She knew he had heard the actual swear word at preschool and was giving it a try at home. He understood that it was not a nice thing to say, but he also wasn't aware of the implications—or even the concept of a curse word.

It was all his mom could do not to burst out laughing.

I'm sorry, but the most adorable four-year-old in the world turning bright red and trying to cuss (but failing miserably) is pretty funny. She held it together, explained to him that he should never say that word again, and put him in time-out for his disrespect. It was incredibly easy to forgive him and let it go because he's so cute and because she loves him and has walked with him in all his struggles. She couldn't imagine him experiencing any kind of *wrath* for his sin.

The question is, if this mother can forgive her child so easily and without any kind of sacrifice or payment, why can't God do that? Isn't God morally superior to her? Isn't he morally superior to me when I forgive *my* kids? Why did he have to punish someone for our sins? Why his own Son?

The reality is that the sins of my friend's son actually *didn't* go unpunished. Even though she forgave him and let it go, there was damage done. *Every sin causes damage, and someone pays for the damage every single time.* In this case, she made *him* pay for the damage by putting him in time-out. If she had let him off the hook, the damage would still be paid for one way or another. Either she would pay by absorbing his insult, or he would pay by not learning his lesson, and perhaps calling his teacher a "bit" and finding himself in the principal's office, feeling ashamed and confused. If she simply forgave him and let him go scot-free, she would be no different than a codependent parent who enables her children to continue to do wrong.

Philosopher and seminary professor Dr. R. Scott Smith made this point in his analysis of progressive theology about the Cross. Commenting on McLaren's rejection of substitutionary atonement, he wrote,

> McLaren's God strikes me as an enabler with poor boundaries, who will let virtually anyone into his family. . . .
>
> No matter how good and helpful they may seem, enablers are not moral heroes. . . .
>
> I don't think we really want such a deficient God. Deep down, I think we want a God who is worthy of worship—who is perfect, not lacking in any good quality, pure in love, compassion, grace, and mercy, but also all-powerful, all-knowing, and holy, just, good, and in control, so that one day he will make right every wrong and deal decisively with, and even eradicate, evil. But McLaren's God cannot deal in any final way with evil. He simply allows evil to continue.[23]

Simply put, without the wrath of God toward sin, heaven would be full of hell.

God's Whipping Boy?

In his book *The Reason Why Faith Makes Sense*, Mark Mittelberg points out that in medieval times, a "whipping boy" was a slave who was brought in to be whipped when a royal prince broke the rules. The prince's tutor couldn't beat the prince himself because he was royalty, so the prince had to watch while a slave was punished in his place. This would purportedly pay the price for the transgression and discourage the prince from doing it again.[24] But is *this* the picture of the Cross the Bible paints for us?

Absolutely not, and here's why: Jesus isn't some hapless victim or uninvolved bystander with no control over his fate. *Jesus is God. He is the one we have sinned against.* And he willingly came to lay down his life for us. In John's Gospel he said, "No one takes [my life] from me, but I lay it down of my own accord. I have authority to lay it down, and I have authority to take it up again. This charge I have received from my Father" (John 10:18). Jesus is not God's whipping boy. Jesus is God in human flesh, and he loved the world so much that he voluntarily came to take the punishment for our sins upon himself.

Think about it this way: Those who denounce God's wrath or accuse the biblical God of being a moral monster are often the very same people who complain that he allows suffering and evil in the world. Yet Scripture tells us of a God who not only gives us an answer for the problem of evil but literally *becomes* the answer. God looked on the evil and sin of the world, stepped into his own creation, and took our sins upon himself to effectively *end* sin and evil forever.

A God who is just and holy cannot simply let sin go—that is plain common sense. But in addition, both the Old and New Testaments are full of passages on the concepts of sacrifice, God requiring blood, God's wrath for sin, and Jesus paying the penalty for our sin. Hebrews 9:22 tells us plainly, "Without the shedding of blood there is no forgiveness of sins." This is built upon what the law says in Leviticus 17:11: "The life of the flesh is in the blood, and I have given it for you on the altar to make atonement for your souls, for it is the blood that makes atonement by the life."

We can't escape it. For those who try, the Christianity they construct is not the real thing. It's an imitation created in their own image . . . one that a strong bout with suffering or a heavy wind of doubt will knock down.

WWJD?

When I was seeking my own answers about the atonement, I wanted to know what Jesus' view was. Much like I wanted my view of the Bible to be informed by what Jesus taught, I wanted my view to line up with his. What *did* Jesus teach? We established in chapter 9 that as a first-century Jew, Jesus believed that the entire Old Testament, also called the Old Covenant, was the inspired and authoritative word of God. He validated Moses, through whom God spoke to institute the sacrificial system (John 5:46).

The Hebrew word translated into English as "atonement" is the word *kaphar*, which primarily means to cover, cleanse, and purify. But this idea was modeled and introduced long before Moses. After committing the first sin, Adam and Eve instantly realized they were naked, felt ashamed, and hid from God. God *covered* them with animal skins from the first blood sacrifice in history. The blood of an innocent animal was shed on behalf of Adam and Eve.

God promised that the offspring of the woman would be stricken but that he would also crush the head of the enemy (Genesis 3:14-15). Soon after, he covered the couple with garments made of skins (verse 21).

Later when establishing the old covenant, God required the Israelites to make animal sacrifices to cover, or atone for, their sins. But Hebrews 10 tells us that these sacrifices could not ultimately take away the sins of the people. Who is the offspring of Adam and Eve who would be stricken? We can look to the book of Isaiah for our answer:

> Surely he has borne our griefs
>   and carried our sorrows;
> yet we esteemed him stricken,
>   smitten by God, and afflicted.
> But he was pierced for our transgressions;
>   he was crushed for our iniquities;
> upon him was the chastisement that brought us peace,
>   and with his wounds we are healed.
> All we like sheep have gone astray;
>   we have turned—every one—to his own way;
> and the LORD has laid on him
>   the iniquity of us all . . .
> *Yet it was the will of the LORD to crush him;*
>   *he has put him to grief;*
> *when his soul makes an offering for guilt,*
>   *he shall see his offspring; he shall prolong his days;*
> *the will of the LORD shall prosper in his hand.*

Out of the anguish of his soul he shall see and be
*   satisfied;*
by his knowledge shall the righteous one, my servant,
*   make many to be accounted righteous,*
*   and he shall bear their iniquities.*
Therefore I will divide him a portion with the many,
*   and he shall divide the spoil with the strong,*
because he poured out his soul to death
*   and was numbered with the transgressors;*
yet he bore the sin of many,
*   and makes intercession for the transgressors.*
ISAIAH 53:4-6, 10-12, EMPHASIS ADDED

This is one of the prophecies that led the Israelites to look for a Messiah . . . one who would bear their sins and make atonement for them with God. Notice the language in this passage: "It was the will of the LORD to crush him." In Acts 2:23, Peter affirmed that Jesus' being delivered up was "according to the definite plan and foreknowledge of God." In other words, the Messiah wouldn't be crucified only because of an angry mob but also because it was God's will. And because of this promised Messiah, Isaiah says many would "be accounted righteous." That means his righteousness would be credited to their account. In other words, their sins would be paid for. (Written about 700 years before Christ, Isaiah is one of the places where the "penal" part of substitutionary atonement is discussed. Contrary to what many progressives repeat over and over, penal substitutionary atonement wasn't invented in the eleventh century.)

With these passages in mind, let's go back to the night before Jesus died to see how he viewed the Cross. In the upper room, Jesus broke bread with his disciples, saying, "This is my body, which is given for you." Then he took the cup of wine and said, "This cup that is poured out for you is the new covenant in my blood" (Luke 22:19-20). Right then and there Jesus was comparing what his death would accomplish with what the sacrificial death of animals accomplished in the old covenant. He was instituting the new covenant.

Later that same night, Jesus quoted directly from Isaiah 53, saying, "For I tell you that this Scripture must be fulfilled in me: 'And he was numbered with the transgressors.' For what is written about me has its fulfillment" (Luke 22:37). Jesus couldn't have been any clearer. The prophecy about the Messiah that spoke of God laying the sins of us all upon him *was about Jesus.*

Jesus saw himself as the ultimate sacrificial lamb. The writer of Hebrews confirms what Jesus was saying: "He entered once for all into the holy places, not by means of the blood of goats and calves but by means of his own blood, thus securing an eternal redemption. . . . He has appeared once for all at the end of the ages to put away sin by the sacrifice of himself" (Hebrews 9:12, 26).

These are some of the many reasons that Christians, for two thousand years, have affirmed that Jesus died for our sins. For some, this sounds like really bad news. But I suppose it all comes down to whether or not you really think you are a sinner. If you think you are basically good and kind and moral, then someone dying an agonizing and bloody death on your behalf sounds horrific and unnecessary. But if you *know* you are a sinner who deserves to pay the ultimate penalty for your sins, as I do, this is the greatest news you could ever receive.

Progressive Christians assume they are painting God in a more tolerant light by denying the substitutionary atonement of Jesus. But in reality, they are simply constructing a codependent and impotent god who is powerless to stop evil. That god is not really good. That god is not the God of the Bible.

That god cannot save you.

12

Reconstruction

*I don't think faith equals a set of propositions,
and in fact, if you go back to the Gospels, I mean,
Jesus never asked anyone to believe anything as a
propositional truth about God, or heaven, or whatever.
Jesus called people to a way of life. He said: "Follow me,
be my disciples." And it was to a way of life, a way of
being in the world. That is a different thing to faith
defined as a set of intellectual propositions.*

Dave Tomlinson

I remember almost nothing about that day. I was driving somewhere for some reason, but I recall only two things about that trip: sunshine and that voice on the radio. It might have been just weeks before that I'd sung those hymns into the thick of darkness and cried into the silent void, asking God to show himself. Maybe it had been months. Was it autumn? I think so, but I don't really know. When you're drowning, you don't tend to look at the calendar.

So many details about those months never made their way into my stored memories. The earliest weeks of my son's life. A body left broken from childbirth. A broken soul. Exhaustion.

And then light.

I do know that the sun was shining that day. I can still feel the warmth radiating through the windshield and diffusing onto my face. And that voice. I'm not a radio person. Never have been. But on this day, I turned on the car radio and pressed Scan. Station after station unleashed its annoyingly shallow junk-pop like a court jester playing the wise fool at a medieval feast. Even the troubadours had nothing for me.

And then the voice. Branded into my memory is the calm, kind, and intelligent voice of a man who was answering questions on a secular college campus. One after another, students hurled their best skeptical objections against Christianity—each one thinking they had finally come up with *the* question that would stump the speaker and bury religion in its grave for good. One by one with skillful precision, he wisely and logically answered them with the tranquil tone of a person who has heard the question a thousand times before. Nearly every one of the clever arguments the progressive pastor had wielded in class was answered with crystal clear common sense.

It was as if a lifeboat had come zooming toward me, with the captain shouting, "There are answers! Get in the boat! There are answers!"

If you also feel as if you are losing your mooring because of deep hurt, doubt, or a progressive's persuasive-sounding arguments, please hear me: There. Are. Answers. I began uncovering them by listening to the daily radio broadcast of a gifted apologist. As the mom of a newborn and a toddler, I didn't have much time to read. But I could listen. So every day while washing dishes, changing diapers, making baby food, driving, or doing laundry, I listened to his program.

Then I discovered other apologetic resources—apps, blogs, and podcasts—that answered so many of my questions. (See the resource section beginning on page 245 for a list of some of them.) As the years went by, my children didn't listen to Barney the purple dinosaur or kids' pop CDs as we ran errands. They were overhearing lectures on genetic entropy, creation versus evolution, and textual criticism. Often their background noise was expository sermons and audiobooks about the historical reliability of the Gospels, church history, and theology. (Maybe this is why my now almost-teenage daughter just asked if I would buy her a T-shirt that says, "Having a weird mom builds character.") After my kids got a little older, I started reading everything I could get my hands on and auditing seminary classes.

Slowly and steadily, God began to rebuild my faith. The questions that had knocked the foundation out from under my beliefs—the ones I had never thought to ask, the ones I didn't know existed—were not simply being answered. They were being dwarfed by substantial evidence and impenetrable logic so robust that I felt like a kid in a candy store—who had just found out that candy exists. Yet each time a question was answered, ten new ones took its place. The process was not quick.

Standing Stronger than Ever

Lest you wonder whether my kids ever had any fun, I have another confession to make: One of my secret joys is building LEGO sets with them. It doesn't matter what we're building,

I just enjoy the whole process—the instructions, the endless hunt for those tiny last pieces, the thrill of the finished work. My daughter and I once spent days assembling a LEGO dragon with a long swooping tail and a fierce, sharp-toothed smirk. It was one of the most intricate sets we'd ever built, mostly because of all the twists and turns in the dragon's body. When we finished the creation, she proudly displayed it on the top of her bookshelf.

Later that day, I walked into her room, only to find her dragon on the floor with its tail severed and dozens of pieces broken off its torso. It looked as if it had fallen and then been stepped on—and then run over by a car. To this day we don't know what happened, except that *maaaaybe* it involved a dog or a little brother or some magical elves. We won't speculate beyond that. But we had a choice to make. Should we scrap the dragon, break it apart, and toss the pieces into the ginormous bin that holds the remains of many busted and discarded LEGO sets? Should we assume that we must have been working from a faulty manual? If so, should we simply toss out the guide and create something new? Or should we carefully gather up the pieces, assess the damage, study the manual, figure out our new starting point, and start building again?

We would have broken most other sets apart and tossed the pieces into the LEGO bin of doom. But this set was different. It meant something to us both. She had waited a long time and worked very hard to earn it, and together we had worked extra hard to construct it. We decided to go back as far as we needed to and rebuild. To find a good starting point, we had to break even more pieces off the dragon's body to reveal the inside, where many stabilizing blocks were lodged. We inspected every block, assessed whether or not it was supposed to be a part of the configuration, and checked to make sure it was in the right place. We discovered that we had missed a step early on, which had weakened the overall structure. This was a flaw we couldn't see once it had all been put together. We had to go back to nearly the beginning and, with great care and attention to detail, rebuild the dragon. Once that correction had been made, the dragon not only looked right, but it was also built right—sturdy and beautiful. Turns out, the manual wasn't flawed . . . our craftsmanship was. And when we finished the dragon for the second time, we treasured it even more because of the extra sweat and tears that had gone into it.

One day as I admired the restored dragon on my daughter's shelf, I realized that this was a bit what my personal deconstruction and reconstruction looked like. Before I walked into class, my worldview was like a finished LEGO set that I thought was sturdy and beautiful. Its overall shape was right. It looked like the photo on the box top. My motivation in building it had been true. But when my faith was in crisis, it was as if someone had smashed it on the floor, stepped on it, and run it over. And I had a choice to make.

Imagine the LEGO set is reality. Everyone receives the same set—the same pieces, the same manual, the same photo on the box top. But it's up to each individual what they do with it. You can choose to build it according to the Designer's intent, using the wisdom he provided in his Word—or you can do your own thing. You can even declare that no one designed it—it's just a random box of blocks. You have that choice.

But if the set is true, it can stand up to questioning. Every line in the manual can be scrutinized without threat. And if you choose to build it according to the Designer's intent, you will have a strong and robust structure that the fiercest wind (or little brother) won't be able to demolish. If you believe the truth about reality, your faith will not be misplaced.

Essential Building Blocks

In a LEGO set, not all pieces have the same importance. Some blocks could break off without anyone even noticing. Some you could remove or switch out without changing the overall structure. You could even put a few of the final blocks on backward or on the wrong side without weakening or significantly changing the final product. But those foundational blocks— the ones upon which the rest of the set is built—those are crucial to get right. If you don't put them in the correct place, the structure won't stand or resemble the photo on the box top.

Likewise, as I researched historic Christianity, one of the most important questions I had to answer was this: What building blocks of our faith are the essentials? In other words, which ones are essential for salvation? Do you have to believe in the Trinity to be saved? The Virgin Birth? What if someone puts saving faith in Jesus but has never heard of the Trinity or the Virgin Birth?

If you ask ten Christians what the essentials of the faith are, you are likely to get ten different lists. In researching this chapter, I googled "What are the essentials of Christianity?" and, I kid you not, the five articles that popped up first all had different lists. The article on top listed ten beliefs. The second and third listed seven—but a different seven. The fourth article listed five. The fifth listed five with dozens of subpoints. Some Christians will appeal to the Apostles' or Nicene Creeds. You get the picture.

But aren't all doctrines equally important? I see this claim on social media all the time. Paul the apostle has something to say about this. Remember that early creed in 1 Corinthians 15:3-5 that we talked about in chapter 3? Let's look at it again:

> For I delivered to you as of first importance what
> I also received: that Christ died for our sins in
> accordance with the Scriptures, that he was buried,
> that he was raised on the third day in accordance
> with the Scriptures, and that he appeared to Cephas,
> then to the twelve.

Paul wrote that these beliefs were "of first importance." That means they were more important than others. In fact, they were the most important ones. These essential beliefs united Christians everywhere. Every Christian affirmed them. I found myself with a good starting point regarding essentials. But surely this isn't enough. This creed says nothing about the deity of Jesus. It doesn't mention monotheism or the Virgin Birth. It doesn't touch on the sinlessness of Christ or his second coming. What was I to make of this?

This is a question that led scholar Dr. Norman Geisler

to study the essentials in regard to salvation. He spent years studying the question, What must one affirm in order to be saved? He studied the question biblically and traced it through church history. I'll do my best to summarize his view, but for the whole enchilada, definitely pick up his systematic theology volume on sin and salvation.[1]

First, Geisler acknowledged that this question could be answered a bit differently throughout world history. Today we have God's written Word—his final revelation. Abraham didn't know everything God would reveal to Moses. Moses didn't have access to the Gospel of John. Yet Old Testament believers were saved in the same way we are now: by grace through faith. Genesis 15:6 tells us that Abraham believed, and it was accounted to him as righteousness. Even though he may not have been aware of the finer workings of the Trinity or Christ's priestly intercession, he was saved by grace through faith.

Today we have God's final revelation, and Geisler concluded that, according to the New Testament, the essentials one must believe (at least implicitly) in order to be saved today are

1. human depravity (I am a sinner);
2. God's unity (There is one God);
3. the necessity of grace (I am saved by grace);
4. Christ's deity (Christ is God);
5. Christ's humanity (Christ is man);
6. Christ's atoning death (Christ died for my sins);
7. Christ's bodily resurrection (Christ rose from the dead); and
8. the necessity of faith (I must believe).[2]

So for people to call themselves Christians, they must at least implicitly believe these eight things. (Notice how closely these align with the essentials embraced by the early church, which we examined on pages 31–33.) There are certainly more truths about God that must exist in order for these eight beliefs to be possible. For example, if Christians have put saving faith in Jesus but haven't heard of the Virgin Birth, they aren't disqualified from salvation. But if they are truly saved, they won't be able to deny the Virgin Birth (essential because it points to Christ's deity) once they gain a bit more knowledge. This may seem like a lot, but it really isn't. We haven't even touched on women in ministry, the age of the earth, or the continuation or cessation of the gifts of the Spirit. That's because those types of doctrines, while not unimportant (I have opinions!), are not *essential*. Christians should not divide over them. Should they robustly debate them? Yes. Should they argue for their view? Absolutely.

But what about the Bible? Is it necessary to believe the Bible is the inerrant and inspired Word of God in order to be saved? Believing in the Bible isn't what saves you, but the gospel can only be fully known if the Bible *actually is* the inerrant and inspired Word of God. The Chicago Statement on Biblical Inerrancy acknowledges that a confession of a belief in inerrancy is not necessary for salvation, but a rejection of it would not come without grave consequences.[3]

Now, are the doctrines I've listed simply "intellectual propositions," as British progressive pastor Dave Tomlinson implies in the quote that opens this chapter? The doctrines themselves might be truths about who God is and how he works in the world, but I agree with Tomlinson that *faith* isn't a set of propositional statements. Faith is trust in a person—Jesus. That trust is based on truth and evidence. You have to know some things about him in order to follow him and trust him. Think about it this way: If you love someone, you want to believe the truth about them. Knowing and believing true things about them does not equal accepting "intellectual propositions," even if they are presented in lists.

If you recognize the truth about yourself, you know how desperately you need God (human depravity). If you cry out for him to save you from your sin (Christ's atoning death) and trust him for your salvation (the necessity of faith), all while knowing deep in your gut that you can't save yourself (the necessity of grace), things get real. These are not intellectual mind games. These beautiful truths about reality usher in the salvation of our souls as our fallen hearts are reconciled to God himself! These "propositions" are exciting news to the desperate sinner. In fact, how can one rightly follow Jesus without knowing who he is and what he accomplished? How can one become a disciple without being taught to understand the gospel?

Insane Beauty

As I took apart my metaphorical LEGO set and put the pieces back together, I discovered that those inner pieces were in the right place. Someone else might deconstruct their set to discover they were missing a core piece or had one in the wrong place. But as I began to put all the blocks back in their rightful places, the finished structure was stronger and more beautiful than ever. Today my faith stands strong against the stormy waves of doubt that challenged the existence of God, the reliability of the Bible, and the truthfulness of Christianity. It looks a little different than it did before, but when I look back on my entire life, I see God's providential hand orchestrating every situation, guiding every step.

The insane beauty of the whole experience is that God led me to the class with the progressive pastor. He knew the end from the beginning. In his unfathomable love and grace, he walked me right into that class and held my hand the whole time. I know that if I could look back on every meeting and every dark moment of doubt—every time I flailed my arms to stay above the stormy water—I would see something I didn't see in real time: him. He was there. He never left me. In fact, the only reason I didn't go under the water was because his strong arms kept me afloat. As I cried out for a lifeboat, he was my life jacket.

I can look back on the class now and smile. Sure, there is still the tender sting of remembrance. There is a touch of sadness at the innocence I lost. When I walk now, I limp a little. When I read the Bible, I no longer read with innocent eyes not yet clouded by skepticism and doubt. But I'd rather walk with a limp on solid ground than run with strong legs on breaking ice. My song has changed, too, as I have found beauty in the struggle:

You made me poor so you could show me that you're all that I need
You brought me low so I could know you in your suffering
To boast in nothing but my weakness you broke my heart to make it clean
Your grace is enough for me

You let the fiery arrows singe me to make beauty from the ash
You let my faith be all but trampled so it would rise from the dust
You set my foolish heart to wander to know how high and far and deep
Your grace is enough for me

You let me stumble in the waiting so my strength could be made new
Confounded all my worldly wisdom so I could be a fool for you
You let me crawl across a desert so I would know that I am free
Your grace is enough for me

The strength of evidence for the Christian worldview is so strong that one would have to willfully shut their eyes to it. But discovering that information takes time and effort and determination. Learning logic and philosophy is not easy. Examining the evidence and digging for truth takes mental energy. Studying the Bible can be daunting and confusing. But isn't every treasure worth the hunt? I found the search exhilarating, catching glimpses of the living God in the writings of Christians who lived centuries ago. It was exciting to discover that a detailed scholarly examination of the Christian worldview only lends support to its veracity. There's nothing better than feeling that your life and your family's life are planted deeply in the truth of Scripture.

Now I consider it a privilege to invite everyone I know on that journey of discovering God's grace because it reaps immense rewards in people's lives. I have seen it with my own eyes.

But while God's grace is free, it does not come cheap. German theologian and martyr Dietrich Bonhoeffer once wrote,

> Cheap grace is the preaching of forgiveness without requiring repentance, baptism without church discipline, Communion without confession, absolution without personal confession. Cheap grace is grace without discipleship, grace without the cross, grace without Jesus Christ, living and incarnate. . . .
>
> Costly grace is the gospel which must be *sought* again and again. . . .
>
> It is *costly* because it cost God the life of his Son: "ye were bought at a price," and what has cost God much cannot be cheap for us. Above all, it is *grace* because God did not reckon his Son too dear a price to pay for our life, but delivered him up for us. Costly grace is the Incarnation of God.[4]

Bonhoeffer lived out these words as he was marched to his death and was hung by the Nazis. His final words were, "This is the end. For me, the beginning of life."[5] He understood what it meant to deny himself, take up his cross, and follow Jesus. He saw the beauty in the gospel.

Everything to Lose

Famous atheist Christopher Hitchens was once interviewed for *Portland Monthly* about his opposition to religion, and more specifically, Christianity. The minister questioning him noted that the Christianity he opposed in one of his best-selling books was of the "fundamentalist" variety, while she identified herself as a "liberal Christian." After explaining that she didn't take the stories in Scripture literally and rejected the atonement, she asked Hitchens if he saw a difference between fundamentalist faith and more liberal (perhaps we could say "progressive") religion. His answer was surprising: "I would say that if you don't believe that Jesus of Nazareth was the Christ and Messiah, and that he rose again from the dead and by his sacrifice our sins are forgiven, you're really not in any meaningful sense a Christian."[6]

I agree with Hitchens. If I became convinced that Christianity was not true, I would not become a progressive Christian. If I became persuaded that the resurrection of Jesus never happened, or that he was simply a good teacher or wise man to imitate, I would not adopt the progressive Christian view of the gospel, the Cross, or the Bible. I would simply walk away from the faith. Because progressive Christianity offers me nothing of value. It gives no hope for the afterlife and no joy in this one. It offers a hundred denials with nothing concrete to affirm.

When I go back in my mind to that moment in the rocking chair—to the darkness and silence—I wonder, *Why was I so upset? Why did it trouble my soul so deeply to think that*

Christianity might not be true? Why would I have felt despondent if I discovered I had lived a lie? Why couldn't I just walk away and move on? I've asked myself these questions dozens of times. The answer is simple. The anguish of my soul was so profound because what I stood to lose was so substantial. If I believed Scripture was only a story ancient people told themselves about God, I would lose the living words of God. That's where I learned who God was, why he came to this earth, and the lengths he went to save me.

I've spilled much ink in this book discussing what's wrong with progressive Christianity and how it differs from historic Christianity, but at the end of the day, progressive Christians are the ones who have everything to lose.

I was so disturbed of heart because I stood to lose God. The consuming fire who spoke creation into existence and yet identifies himself as Father. I stood to lose Jesus, the Messiah predicted by the Old Testament prophets and trumpeted after four hundred years of divine silence as the "Lamb of God, who takes away the sin of the world" (John 1:29). I stood to lose my Savior. The assurance that my sins had been paid for—that I had been bought with a price. That he died in my place. I stood to lose the beauty of the gospel. I stood to lose the confidence that everything wrong in this wretched world will one day be made right. I stood to lose the hope of no more tears, no more crying, no more pain. I stood to lose the mysterious stability of God's written Word. The lamp to my feet. The light to my path.

We don't get to completely redefine who God is and how he works in the world and call it Christian. We don't get to make the rules and do what is right in our own eyes and yet claim to be followers of Jesus. Our only option is to do it his way or not at all. He is love. His name is truth. His gospel is bloody. His way is beautiful. For God so loved the world.

I want to join my voice with the saints who've gone before me. I want to unite with Peter and Paul, Athanasius, Ignatius, and Augustine. I want to worship with Aquinas, Spurgeon, and Tozer. I want to stand beside my husband, my kids, and all those whom God will save to sing praises to our Creator. My earnest hope and prayer is to see you—my reader—on that glorious day too, forgiven, washed pure, standing firm on what is true, and enjoying the immense beauty of it all. We'll join our voices together with countless saints from every tribe, nation, and tongue—every creature in heaven and earth and under the earth and sea:

> Worthy is the Lamb who was slain,
> to receive power and wealth and wisdom and might
> and honor and glory and blessing! . . .
> To him who sits on the throne and to the Lamb
> be blessing and honor and glory and might forever
> and ever![7]

Amen!

Acknowledgments

My family and friends:

Mike, thank you for loving me and being my biggest supporter and cheerleader. You live out Ephesians 5:25 every single day. Mychael and Wyatt, thank you for accepting me into your family and letting me be a part of your lives. Your presence in my life has deepened me and taught me so much about love. Dyllan and Ayden, there's nothing I wouldn't do for you. My greatest prayer is that you will love Jesus and walk with him all the days of your life. I love you all with my whole heart.

My sisters, Kristin, Cherie, and Nikki, thank you for being my growing-up pals, my closest friends, and the ones who understand me best. Thank you to my nieces and nephews, Lauren, Ryan, Kailyn, Leona, Ava, and Charlize, for bringing unimaginable joy to my life. Matthew, your very existence has been an indescribable gift. Our hearts are crushed in your absence, but we will see you again. In that, you have taught me what it means to have hope. Clyde, Thelma, Mark, and Ivey, thank you for your love.

Teasi Cannon, Carianne Long, Michelle Bagnasco, Chrissy Katina, Kristin Schweain, Amber Brandt, Elizabeth Stewart, and Tammy Trent, your friendships have meaningfully shaped my life at different times and in various seasons.

Diane Woerner, you've been in the trenches with me for the last few years, reading, editing, encouraging, pushing back, or smoothing out my blog posts. My editor and friend. (I left that last sentence purposely incomplete in honor of the hours we spent deciding whether incomplete sentences worked for a certain emphasis or were simply bad grammar.)

My apologetics community:

Frank Turek and J. Warner Wallace, you were the first "big time" apologists to encourage me to pursue this path. You believed I had something to bring to the table, and it was your mentorship, instruction, and wise counsel that helped lead me here.

Eric Gustafson, Adam Tucker, and everyone at Southern Evangelical Seminary, thank you for accepting me into your family although I didn't even take my classes for credit! Your heart to help a stay-at-home mom with her doubts and questions is something I will never forget. I thank God for you.

Others who played an instrumental role in encouraging me throughout this process are Hillary Ferrer and all the other Mama Bears, David Young, Michael Goff, Jonathan Morrow, Mark Mittelberg, Greg Koukl, Brett Kunkle, Rebekah and

ACKNOWLEDGMENTS

Richard Howe, Scott Williamson, Jan Williamson, everyone at Women in Apologetics, Amy Hall, Tim Barnett, Jorge Gil, Sean McDowell, Bobby Conway, Jay Strother, and countless others whose books, blogs, and podcasts were like lifeboats when my faith was going under. Natasha Crain, if you hadn't strongly encouraged me to write this book, it might not have happened. Thank you for the push. Mr. Weitzel, my seventh and twelfth grade English teacher, you caused me to love writing and somehow made me believe I could do it.

To all the scholars and smart friends who were available to review everything from single paragraphs to entire chapters for accuracy—Dr. Mel Winstead, Dr. Peter J. Williams, Dr. Peter Gurry, Dr. Patrick Sawyer, Clark Bates, Dr. R. Scott Smith, Clay Jones, Jean E. Jones, and Benjamin J. Nickodemus—I am deeply indebted to you.

The publishing team:

Ron Beers and everyone at Tyndale, thank you for believing in this book. Jon Farrar, thank you for your constant encouragement, support, editing, and feedback. Kim Miller and Annette Hayward, thank you for your steadfast attention to detail, relentless fact-checking, tireless research, and wholehearted investment in making this book everything it could be. Kara Leonino and Jillian Schlossberg, thanks for your help in shepherding this book through the publishing process. Eva Winters, I'm grateful for the artistry you brought to the design of the book's cover and interior.

My agent, Bill Jensen: Almost no one is more responsible

for making this happen than you. From talking with you on the phone for the first time while I was in Costco to fishing on the McKenzie River to embarrassing myself gorging on your irresistible grilled vegetables, you and Sheila have become family. Your fingerprints are all over this book, and I'm so grateful for your guidance (both spiritual and literary) and your unwavering commitment to providing the body of Christ with resources that help them discern the real gospel versus another gospel.

Additional Resources

Books

Apologetics

Craig, William Lane. *Reasonable Faith: Christian Truth and Apologetics*, 3rd ed. Wheaton, IL: Crossway, 2008.

Geisler, Norman, and Frank Turek. *I Don't Have Enough Faith to Be an Atheist*. Wheaton, IL: Crossway, 2004.

Habermas, Gary R., and Michael R. Licona. *The Case for the Resurrection of Jesus*. Grand Rapids, MI: Kregel, 2004.

Keller, Timothy. *Making Sense of God: Finding God in the Modern World*. New York: Penguin Books, 2016.

Keller, Timothy. *The Reason for God: Belief in an Age of Skepticism*. New York: Penguin Books, 2008.

Koukl, Greg. *Tactics: A Game Plan for Discussing Your Christian Convictions*, 10th anniversary ed. Grand Rapids, MI: Zondervan, 2018.

Lewis, C. S. *Mere Christianity*. New York: HarperCollins, 2015.

Strobel, Lee. *The Case for Christ: A Journalist's Personal Investigation of the Evidence for Jesus*. Grand Rapids, MI: Zondervan, 1998.

Wallace, J. Warner. *Cold-Case Christianity: A Homicide Detective Investigates the Claims of the Gospels*. Colorado Springs: David C. Cook, 2013.

Wright, N. T. *The Resurrection of the Son of God*. Minneapolis: Fortress, 2003.

The Bible/New Testament Documents

Bauckham, Richard. *Jesus and the Eyewitnesses: The Gospels as Eyewitness Testimony*. Grand Rapids, MI: Eerdmans, 2017.

Bruce, F. F. *The New Testament Documents*, 6th ed. Grand Rapids, MI: Eerdmans, 1981.

Gallagher, Edmon L., and John D. Meade. *The Biblical Canon Lists from Early Christianity: Texts and Analysis*. Oxford, UK: Oxford University Press, 2017.

Geisler, Norman L., and Thomas A. Howe. *The Big Book of Bible Difficulties: Clear and Concise Answers from Genesis to Revelation*. Grand Rapids, MI: Baker, 1992.

Geisler, Norman, and William E. Nix. *A General Introduction to the Bible*. Chicago: Moody, 1986.

Gurry, Peter J., and Elijah Hixson, eds. *Myths and Mistakes in New Testament Textual Criticism*. Downers Grove, IL: IVP Academic, 2019.

Kruger, Michael. *The Question of Canon: Challenging the Status Quo in the New Testament Debate.* Downers Grove, IL: IVP Academic, 2013.

Williams, Peter J. *Can We Trust the Gospels?* Wheaton, IL: Crossway, 2018.

Wilson, Andrew. *Unbreakable: What the Son of God Said about the Word of God.* La Grange, KY: 10Publishing, 2014.

Devotional/Christian Living

Augustine. *The Confessions.* Oxford, UK: Oxford University Press, 1992.

Bonhoeffer, Dietrich. *The Cost of Discipleship.* New York: Touchstone, 1995.

Chesterton, G. K. *Orthodoxy.* New York: Penguin, 1991.

Guinness, Os. *The Call: Finding and Fulfilling the Central Purpose of Your Life.* Nashville: Thomas Nelson, 2003.

Packer, J. I. *Knowing God.* Downers Grove, IL: IVP, 1973.

Tozer, A. W. *The Pursuit of God.* Ventura, CA: Regal, 2013.

Tozer, A. W. *Voice of a Prophet: Who Speaks for God?* Bloomington, MN: Bethany House, 2014.

Historic Christianity/Theology

Berkhof, Louis. *The History of Christian Doctrines.* Carlisle, PA: Banner of Truth, 1996.

Craig, William Lane. *The Atonement*. Cambridge, UK: Cambridge University Press, 2018.

Evans, Craig A. *Fabricating Jesus: How Modern Scholars Distort the Gospels*. Downers Grove, IL: IVP, 2009.

Gathercole, Simon. *Defending Substitution: An Essay on Atonement in Paul*. Grand Rapids, MI: Baker Academic, 2015.

Keener, Craig S. *The Historical Jesus of the Gospels*. Grand Rapids, MI: Eerdmans, 2009.

Köstenberger, Andreas J., and Michael J. Kruger. *The Heresy of Orthodoxy: How Contemporary Culture's Fascination with Diversity Has Reshaped Our Understanding of Early Christianity*. Wheaton, IL: Crossway, 2010.

Kruger, Michael J. *Christianity at the Crossroads: How the Second Century Shaped the Future of the Church*. Downers Grove, IL: IVP, 2018.

Machen, J. Gresham. *Christianity and Liberalism*. Louisville, KY: GLH Publishing, 1923.

Schaff, Philip, ed. *The Complete Ante-Nicene & Nicene and Post-Nicene Church Fathers Collection*. London: Catholic Way Publishing, 2014.

Shelley, Bruce L. *Church History in Plain Language*, 4th ed. Nashville: Thomas Nelson, 2013.

Shenvi, Neil, and Pat Sawyer. *Engaging Critical Theory and the Social Justice Movement*. Ratio Christi, 2019.

Smith, R. Scott. *Authentically Emergent: In Search of a Truly Progressive Christianity*. Eugene, OR: Cascade, 2018.

Sexual Ethics

Allberry, Sam. *Is God Anti-Gay? And Other Questions about Homosexuality, the Bible and Same-Sex Attraction.* Charlotte, NC: The Good Book Co., 2013.

Butterfield, Rosaria Champagne. *The Secret Thoughts of an Unlikely Convert: An English Professor's Journey into Christian Faith.* Pittsburgh: Crown & Covenant Publishing, 2012.

Cook, Becket. *A Change of Affection: A Gay Man's Incredible Story of Redemption.* Nashville: Thomas Nelson, 2019.

DeYoung, Kevin. *What Does the Bible Really Teach about Homosexuality?* Wheaton, IL: Crossway, 2015.

Gagnon, Robert A. J. *The Bible and Homosexual Practice: Texts and Hermeneutics.* Nashville: Abingdon Press, 2001.

Yuan, Christopher. *Holy Sexuality and the Gospel: Sex, Desire, and Relationships Shaped by God's Grand Story.* Colorado Springs: Multnomah, 2018.

Yuan, Christopher. *Out of a Far Country: A Gay Son's Journey to God. A Broken Mother's Search for Hope.* Colorado Springs: WaterBrook, 2011.

Podcasts

The Alisa Childers Podcast

The Bible Recap

Bible Thinker with Mike Winger

The Cold-Case Christianity Podcast with J. Warner Wallace

Defenders Podcast with William Lane Craig

I Don't Have Enough Faith to Be an Atheist with Frank Turek

Mama Bear Apologetics Podcast

The Naked Bible Podcast with Michael Heiser

Reasonable Faith Podcast with William Lane Craig

RZIM podcasts: *Ask Away*; *The Defense Rests*; *Just Thinking*; *Let My People Think*

Stand to Reason with Greg Koukl

Why Do You Believe?, the official podcast of Southern Evangelical Seminary

Discussion Guide

1. Have you or someone close to you ever gone through "spiritual labor"? If so, how would you describe the process? The outcome?

2. Alisa describes her faith as intellectually weak and untested before she began the class with the progressive pastor (see page 5). In what ways may your faith be vulnerable to questions, doubts, or temptations?

3. As Alisa discovered, being faithful to God doesn't mean we can never question parts of our faith tradition. As an example, she describes her unease with some types of altar calls. Is there anything in your religious tradition that has given you pause?

4. Deconstruction is the process of "systematically dissecting and often rejecting the beliefs you grew up with" (see page 24). In what ways can this process be healthy? Unhealthy?

5. Why do you think so many people are drawn to progressive Christianity?

6. In chapter 4, Alisa unpacks a number of factors that lead people to begin to question their faith: abuse within the church; doubts that are discouraged or dismissed; the moral demands of historic Christianity; misgivings about the Bible; secular philosophies (like critical theory); legalism; and the problem of suffering. Have any of these have affected your faith? If so, how? What other factors may cause people to question their beliefs?

7. As you look around our church culture, do you think people are more likely to add to or subtract from the gospel message? Explain.

8. Do you agree that progressive Christianity employs a form of what C. S. Lewis called "chronological snobbery" (see page 109)? Why or why not?

9. Have you ever had questions about the Bible that have caused you to doubt its reliability? If so, what are they? How does Alisa's research address those questions?

10. After reading this book, what would you say to a friend who asks why we can trust the testimony of the four Gospels?

11. Why do you think hell is such an uncomfortable topic for many people? Has your understanding of it changed after reading chapter 10? If so, how?

12. Alisa suggests that progressives have a distorted view of the God who reveals himself in the Bible. Do you agree? If so, in what ways would you say he is portrayed inaccurately by progressive Christians?

13. How do you reconcile God's wrath with his loving kindness?

14. For which questions or doubts have you found answers in this book? What steps will you take going forward in an attempt to resolve any remaining questions you have about your Christian faith?

About the Author

ALISA CHILDERS is a wife, a mom, an author, a blogger, a speaker, and a worship leader. She was a member of the award-winning CCM recording group ZOEgirl. She is a popular speaker at apologetics and Christian worldview conferences, including STR's Reality Conference. Alisa has been published at The Gospel Coalition, The Christian Post, Crosswalk, The Stream, For Every Mom, and *Decision* magazine. Her blog post "Girl, Wash Your Face? What Rachel Hollis Gets Right . . . and Wrong" received more than one million views. You can connect with Alisa online at alisachilders.com.

Notes

CHAPTER 1: CRISIS OF FAITH
1. Charitie Lees Bancroft, "Before the Throne of God Above," 1863.
2. John Pavlovitz, "Progressive Christianity—Is Christianity," *Stuff That Needs to Be Said* (blog), October 5, 2016, https://johnpavlovitz.com /2016/10/05/explaining-progressive-christianity-otherwise-known-as -christianity/.

CHAPTER 2: THE ROCKS IN MY SHOES
1. Alisa Childers, "I Say," Vintage Street Music, copyright © Alisa Childers 2007.
2. Alisa Childers, "Baptize Me," Vintage Street Music, copyright © Alisa Childers 2007.
3. Brian D. McLaren, *A Generous Orthodoxy* (Grand Rapids, MI: Zondervan, 2004), 44.
4. See my article "3 Beliefs Some Progressive Christians and Atheists Share," The Gospel Coalition, November 13, 2018, https://www.thegospelcoalition .org/article/3-beliefs-progressive-christians-atheists-share/.

CHAPTER 3: CREEDS, COBBLER, AND WALTER BAUER
1. Atheist New Testament scholar Gerd Lüdemann dates it to within two or three years of the Crucifixion. Non-Christian scholar and Jesus Seminar founder Robert Funk and world-renowned New Testament scholar N. T. Wright agree. See Gerd Lüdemann, *The Resurrection of Jesus* (Minneapolis: Fortress Press, 1992), 171–72; Robert Walter Funk and the Jesus Seminar, *The Acts of Jesus* (New York: Polebridge Press, 1998), 466; N. T. Wright, *The Resurrection of the Son of God* (Minneapolis: Fortress Press, 2003), 319.
2. Bart Ehrman, "The Core of Paul's Gospel," *The Bart Ehrman Blog*, June 2, 2016, https://ehrmanblog.org/the-core-of-pauls-gospel/.
3. Ehrman, "The Core of Paul's Gospel."

4. For instance, the first Christians understood that the Old Testament sacrificial system pointed to "Christ, our Passover Lamb" (1 Corinthians 5:7), who took our sin on himself. For other passages they understood to be speaking of Jesus, see Genesis 3:15; Psalm 22:14-18; and Isaiah 53.

5. Habermas points to several passages, including Romans 1:3-4, 10:8-9; 1 Corinthians 8:6; and Philippians 2:6-11. See his book *The Uniqueness of Jesus Christ among the Major World Religions* (self-pub., 2016), 29, http://www.garyhabermas.com/Evidence2/. See also Oscar Cullmann, *The Earliest Christian Confessions*, ed. Gary Habermas and Benjamin Charles Shaw, trans. J. K. S. Reid (Eugene, OR: Wipf and Stock, 2018).

6. Pliny the Younger, Book 10, Letter 96.

7. John 8:53, NLT

8. John 8:58, NKJV

9. Exodus 3:14, NKJV

10. Thomas 14; 3; 114

11. Michael J. Kruger, "The Heresy of Orthodoxy: Who Is Walter Bauer and Why Write a Book about Him?" Canon Fodder, November 6, 2017, https://www.michaeljkruger.com/the-heresy-of-orthodoxy-who-is-walter-bauer-and-why-write-a-book-about-him/.

12. See Andreas J. Köstenberger and Michael J. Kruger, *The Heresy of Orthodoxy: How Contemporary Culture's Fascination with Diversity Has Reshaped Our Understanding of Early Christianity* (Wheaton, IL: Crossway, 2010) and my article "When Was the New Testament Considered Scripture? 5 Facts That Point to an Early Canon," January 16, 2017, https://www.alisachilders.com/blog/when-was-the-new-testament-considered-scripture-5-facts-that-point-to-an-early-canon.

13. J. Warner Wallace has done extensive work analyzing the content, dating, and theological presuppositions of the noncanonical gospels, in the form of articles and podcasts. See, for example, "A Thorough Guide to the Non-Canonical Gospels," *Cold-Case Christianity* (blog), January 17, 2018, https://coldcasechristianity.com/writings/a-thorough-guide-to-the-non-canonical-gospels/.

14. Wallace, "A Thorough Guide to the Non-Canonical Gospels."

15. Norman L. Geisler and Frank Turek, *I Don't Have Enough Faith to Be an Atheist* (Wheaton, IL: Crossway, 2004), 364, 586–87.

16. Nadia Bolz-Weber, *Shameless: A Sexual Reformation* (New York: Convergent, 2019), 189–95; House for All Sinners and Saints website, http://houseforall.org/whoweare/.

17. Lisa Gray, "Nadia Bolz-Weber Urges Christians to Be 'Shameless' in Their Sexuality," February 15, 2019, *Houston Chronicle*, https://www.houstonchronicle.com/life/houston-belief/article/Nadia-Bolz-Weber-urges-Christians-to-be-13619448.php.

NOTES

CHAPTER 4: FIXING WHAT ISN'T BROKEN

1. Kara Powell, "Steve Jobs, Back to School, and Why Doubt Belongs in Your Youth Group Curriculum," *Christianity Today*, September 2012, https://www.christianitytoday.com/women/2012/september/steve-jobs-back-to-school-and-why-doubt-belongs-in-your.html.

2. The resources on this would be too many to mention here, but a couple of examples are *The Airing of Grief* podcast and *#Exvangelical* podcast.

3. R. Scott Smith, *Authentically Emergent: In Search of a Truly Progressive Christianity* (Eugene, OR: Cascade Books, 2018), 99, emphasis in original.

4. Sam Allberry, *Is God Anti-Gay?: And Other Questions about Homosexuality, the Bible and Same-Sex Attraction* (Charlotte, NC: The Good Book Company, 2015), 11–12, emphasis in original.

5. Rachel Held Evans, *Inspired: Slaying Giants, Walking on Water, and Loving the Bible Again* (Nashville: Thomas Nelson, 2018), xi.

6. Evans, *Inspired*, xii.

7. Clay Jones, "We Don't Hate Sin So We Don't Understand What Happened to the Canaanites," *Philosophia Christi* 11, no. 1 (2009), https://ibs.cru.org/files/5214/3336/7724/We-Dont-Hate-Sin-PC-article.pdf.

8. Paul Copan, *Is God a Moral Monster?: Making Sense of the Old Testament God* (Grand Rapids, MI: Baker Publishing Group, 2011), 175–77.

9. It's not possible to fully explain critical theory here, but for an excellent and expanded treatment of critical theory and Christianity, see Neil Shenvi and Patrick Sawyer, "Engaging Critical Theory and the Social Justice Movement," Ratio Christi, June 5, 2019, https://ratiochristi.org/engaging-critical-theory-and-the-social-justice-movement/.

10. Beverly Daniel Tatum, "The Complexity of Identity: 'Who Am I?,'" *Readings for Diversity and Social Justice*, ed. Maurianne Adams et al. (New York: Routledge, 2000); Özlem Sensoy and Robin DiAngelo, *Is Everyone Really Equal?: An Introduction to Key Concepts in Social Justice Education* (New York: Teachers College Press, 2017).

11. Bradley A. U. Levinson, "Exploring Critical Social Theories and Education," in *Beyond Critique*, ed. Bradley A. U. Levinson (Boulder, CO: Paradigm Publishers, 2011), 2.

12. Pat Sawyer and Neil Shenvi, "Gender, Intersectionality, and Critical Theory," *Eikon* 1, no. 2 (Fall 2019): 74–81 , https://cbmw.org/2019/11/20/gender-intersectionality-and-critical-theory/.

13. Sawyer and Shenvi, "Gender, Intersectionality, and Critical Theory."

14. Jen Hatmaker, Facebook, October 7, 2019, https://www.facebook.com/jenhatmaker/posts/2385914171507564.

15. Sarah Bessey, "Penny in the Air: My Story of Becoming Affirming," SarahBessey.com, June 5, 2019, https://sarahbessey.com/penny-in-the-air-my-story-of-becoming-affirming/.

16. Lexico.com, s.v. "fundamentalism," accessed December 17, 2019, https://www.lexico.com/en/definition/fundamentalism.

CHAPTER 5: A DIFFERENT KIND OF CHRISTIANITY

1. From statement by LeRon Shults in "Doctrinal Statement(?)," Emergent Village, May 4, 2006, https://emergent-us.typepad.com/emergentus/2006/05/doctrinal_state.html.

2. Brian McLaren, "Q & R: Is the Emerging Church Movement Fizzling Out?," BrianMcLaren.net, April 14, 2012, https://brianmclaren.net/q-r-is-the-emerging-church-movement-fizzling-out/.

3. Anne Kennedy, "Answering a Kind Comment," *Preventing Grace with Anne Kennedy* (blog), May 7, 2019, https://www.patheos.com/blogs/preventinggrace/2019/05/07/answering-a-kind-comment/.

4. Brian Mattson, "Sympathy for the Devil," March 31, 2014, http://drbrianmattson.com/journal/2014/3/31/sympathy-for-the-devil.

5. See Tertullian, "The Prescription against Heretics, XXXII," in *The Church Fathers. The Complete Ante-Nicene & Nicene and Post-Nicene Church Fathers Collection: 3 Series, 37 Volumes, 65 Authors, 1,000 Books, 18,000 Chapters, 16 Million Words*, ed. Philip Schaff (London: Catholic Way Publishing, 2014), loc. 49269–71, Kindle.

6. Clement, "The First Epistle of Clement to the Corinthians, XIII, XLV," in *The Church Fathers,* loc. 175211 and 175514–15, Kindle.

7. Justin Martyr, "First Apology, XXXVI" in *The Church Fathers*, loc. 5762, Kindle.

8. Ireneaus, "Against Heresies, 3.3.4" in *The Church Fathers*, loc. 13525, Kindle.

9. Irenaeus, "Against Heresies, 2.28.2" in *The Church Fathers,* loc. 13525, Kindle.

10. Augustine, "Letters, 23.3.3" in *The Church Fathers*, loc. 212108 and 190661, Kindle.

11. Johnny Walsh, "Nadia Bolz-Weber Does Ministry Differently," Out in Jersey, October 21, 2018, https://outinjersey.net/nadia-bolz-weber-does-ministry-differently/.

12. Augustine, "Contra Faustum, Book XVII," in *The Church Fathers*, loc. 248970, Kindle.

13. Clement, "The First Epistle of Clement to the Corinthians, XLIX," in *The Church Fathers,* loc. 2346, Kindle.

14. "Epistle of Barnabas," in *The Church Fathers,* loc. 2551, Kindle.

15. "The Epistle of Mathetes to Diognetus, IX," in *The Church Fathers*, loc. 2555, Kindle.

16. Athanasius of Alexandria, "On the Incarnation." The first sentence comes from the digital edition by Blue Letter Bible, page 7; the second sentence comes from *The Church Fathers,* loc. 493740–41, Kindle; emphasis mine.

NOTES

17. Augustine, "Contra Faustum, Book XIV," in *The Church Fathers*, loc. 248058–59, Kindle, emphasis added.

18. Michael Gungor (@Michael Gungor), Twitter, February 25, 2017, 9:57 a.m., https://twitter.com/michaelgungor/status/835549384079093760.

19. Michael Gungor (@Michael Gungor), Twitter, February 25, 2017, 10:08 a.m., https://twitter.com/michaelgungor/status/835552177582034944?lang=en.

20. Michael Gungor (@Michael Gungor), Twitter, February 26, 2017, 4:31 p.m., https://twitter.com/michaelgungor/status/836010890566725632?lang=en.

21. Brian Zahnd, *Sinners in the Hands of a Loving God: The Scandalous Truth of the Very Good News* (New York: Waterbrook, 2017), 100, Kindle.

22. Augustine, "Contra Faustum, Book XIV," in *The Church Fathers,* loc. 248063–64, Kindle; emphasis mine.

23. See Wayne A. Grudem, *Systematic Theology: An Introduction to Biblical Doctrine* (Grand Rapids, MI: Zondervan, 1994), 490–514, Kindle.

24. Grudem, *Systematic Theology*, 202, Kindle.

25. Michael J. Kruger, *Christianity at the Crossroads: How the Second Century Shaped the Future of the Church* (Downers Grove, IL: IV Press, 2017), 136.

26. Iranaeus wrote, "We refer [the heretics] to that tradition from the apostles which is preserved through the succession of presbyters in the churches."

27. Tertullian, "The Prescription against Heretics," in *The Church Fathers,* loc. 48988–94, Kindle.

28. Kruger, *Christianity at the Crossroads*, 136–37, 143.

29. Kruger, *Christianity at the Crossroads*, 144.

30. Brian McLaren, *A New Kind of Christianity* (San Francisco: HarperOne, 2010), 139, Kindle.

31. St. Irenaeus, *Against Heresies*, ed. Paul A. Böer Sr (n.p.: Veritatis Splendor Publications, 2012), 66, Kindle.

CHAPTER 6: NOTHING NEW UNDER THE SUN

1. Scripture quotations in this paragraph are taken from Matthew 13:36-43, NIV.

2. Craig L. Blomberg, *Interpreting the Parables*, 2nd ed. (Downers Grove, IL: IVP, 2012), 246.

3. John Piper, "Should We Call Out False Teachers or Ignore Them?" Desiring God, October 4, 2019, https://www.desiringgod.org/interviews/should-we-call-out-false-teachers-or-ignore-them.

4. Francis T. Fallon, "The Gnostics: The Undominated Race," *Novum Testamentum* 21, no. 3 (July 1979): 283, https://doi.org/10.2307/1560836.

5. St. Irenaeus, *Against Heresies*, ed. Paul A. Böer Sr. (n.p.: Veritatis Splendor Publications, 2012), 77, Kindle.

6. St. Irenaeus, *Against Heresies*, 29, originally published in "Gnosticism," *The Catholic Encyclopedia* vol. 6 (New York: Robert Appleton Co., 1909).

7. In the introduction to *Against Heresies*, John Arendzen reports that Gnostics had versions of baptism, anointing with oil, and the Eucharist.

8. John Zmirak, "Today's Progressive Christians Are the Best Christians in History. Just Ask Them!," *The Stream*, January 31, 2017, https://stream.org/todays-progressive-christians-best-christians-history-just-ask/.

9. Brian D. McLaren, *A New Kind of Christianity* (San Francisco: HarperOne, 2010), 98.

10. McLaren, *A New Kind of Christianity*, 103.

11. C. S. Lewis, *Surprised by Joy* (New York: Harcourt, Brace, Jovanovich, 1966), 207–8.

12. McLaren, *A New Kind of Christianity*, 278.

13. McLaren, *A New Kind of Christianity*, 98–99.

14. This is the view hinted at in the book *The Shack*, in which the wounds of crucifixion are found on Papa (the Father) as well as on Jesus.

15. Robert Murray M'Cheyne and Andrew Alexander Bonar, *Memoir and Remains of the Rev. Robert Murray M'Cheyne* (Edinburgh: Oliphant, Anderson, and Ferrier, 1883), 64.

CHAPTER 7: FOR THE BIBLE TELLS ME SO?

1. Esther 4:16 (TLB); Ecclesiastes 12:1 (TLB); Song of Solomon 5:9 (TLB)

2. John 19:30

3. Andreas J. Köstenberger and Michael Kruger, *The Heresy of Orthodoxy: How Contemporary Culture's Fascination with Diversity Has Reshaped Our Understanding of Early Christianity* (Wheaton, IL: Crossway, 2010), 197.

4. Charles B. Puskas and C. Michael Robbins, *An Introduction to the New Testament*, 2nd ed. (Eugene, OR: Cascade Books, 2011), 53.

5. "The St. John Fragment, the Earliest Known Fragment from a Papyrus Codex of the New Testament," Jerry Norman's HistoryofInformation.com, http://www.historyofinformation.com/detail.php?id=1410.

6. Elijah Hixson and Peter J. Gurry, eds., *Myths and Mistakes in New Testament Textual Criticism* (Downers Grove, IL: IVP Academic, 2019), 193–94.

7. Bart Ehrman, ""Why Would I Call Myself Both an Agnostic or an Atheist?: A Blast from the Past," *The Bart Ehrman Blog: The History and Literature of Early Christianity*, July 4, 2017, https://ehrmanblog.org/am-i-an-agnostic-or-an-atheist-a-blast-from-the-past/.

8. Bart Ehrman, "New Testament Manuscripts: Good News and Bad News," *The Bart Ehrman Blog: The History and Literature of Early Christianity*, July

18, 2015, https://ehrmanblog.org/new-testament-manuscripts-good-news
-and-bad-news/.

9. Daniel B. Wallace, "My Favorite Passage That's Not in the Bible,"
Disputed New Testament Passages: Textual Criticism Put into Practice,
iTunes U, lecture, June 26, 2011, see track 3 at https://itunes.apple.com
/ua/itunes-u/disputed-new-testament-passages/id446655229?mt=10.

10. Daniel B. Wallace, "My Favorite Passage That's Not in the Bible," Bible.org,
June 25, 2008, https://bible.org/article/my-favorite-passage-thats-not-bible.

11. Robert B. Stewart, ed., *The Reliability of the New Testament: Bart D.
Ehrman and Daniel B. Wallace in Dialogue* (Minneapolis: Fortress, 2011),
12.

12. Bart D. Ehrman, *Misquoting Jesus: The Story behind Who Changed the
Bible and Why* (San Francisco: HarperSanFrancisco, 2005), 7, italics in the
original.

13. Peter Gurry (@pjgurry), "Last night I showed this slide to a group of
Christians," March 9, 2019, 10:46 a.m., https://twitter.com/pjgurry/status
/1104453336638447617?s=21.

CHAPTER 8: WAS IT TRUE ONLY FOR THEM?

1. Holly Ordway, *Not God's Type: An Atheist Academic Lays Down Her Arms*
(San Francisco: Ignatius Press, 2014), 122.

2. Bart Ehrman, *The New Testament: A Historical Introduction to the Early
Christian Writings* (Oxford: Oxford University Press, 1997), 40–41.

3. Peter J. Williams, *Can We Trust the Gospels?* (Wheaton, IL: Crossway,
2018), 49.

4. Peter J. Williams, "Can We Trust the Gospels?" lecture at Second Baptist
Church, Woodway, Texas, April 4, 2014, YouTube video, 1:01:27, https://
www.youtube.com/watch?v=wi2_VNz_pKw.

5. Josephus was a noted first-century Jewish historian who wrote: "But
let not the testimony of women be admitted, on account of the levity
and boldness of their sex, nor let servants be admitted to give testimony
on account of the ignobility of their soul; since it is probable that they
may not speak truth, either out of hope of gain, or fear of punishment"
(Josephus, *Antiquities of the Jews*, 4.8.15). Josephus, Flavius. Josephus
Flavius: Complete Works and Historical Background (Annotated and
Illustrated), loc. 12299, Kindle.

6. J. Warner Wallace, *Cold-Case Christianity: A Homicide Detective Investigates
the Claims of the Gospels* (Colorado Springs: David C. Cook, 2013), 75.

7. Wallace, *Cold-Case Christianity*, 79.

8. For a more thorough survey, see William S. Stob, *The Four Gospels: A*

Guide to Their Historical Background, Characteristic Differences, and Timeless Significance (Greenville, SC: Ambassador International, 2007), loc. 6749, Kindle.

9. *The Church Fathers. The Complete Ante-Nicene & Nicene and Post-Nicene Church Fathers Collection: 3 Series, 37 Volumes, 65 Authors, 1,000 Books, 18,000 Chapters, 16 Million Words* (Kindle Locations 450142–43). Catholic Way Publishing, Kindle.

10. Norman Geisler and Thomas Howe, *When Critics Ask: A Popular Handbook on Bible Difficulties* (Wheaton, IL: Victor Books, 1992). See https://defendinginerrancy.com/bible-solutions/Matthew_21.2_(cf ._Mark_11.2;_Luke_19.30).php.

CHAPTER 9: AUTHORITY PROBLEMS

1. Peter Enns, *The Bible Tells Me So: Why Defending Scripture Has Made Us Unable to Read It* (San Francisco: HarperOne, 2014), 11–12.

2. Enns, *The Bible Tells Me So*, 17.

3. Enns, *The Bible Tells Me So.*

4. Enns, *The Bible Tells Me So.*

5. Rachel Held Evans, *Inspired: Slaying Giants, Walking on Water, and Loving the Bible Again* (Nashville: Thomas Nelson, 2018), xx.

6. Enns, *The Bible Tells Me So*, 231.

7. Brian McLaren, *A New Kind of Christianity* (San Francisco: Harper One, 2010), 103.

8. Brian Zahnd, *Sinners in the Hands of a Loving God* (New York: Crown Publishing, 2017), 30.

9. Richard Rohr, *Falling Upward* (San Francisco: Jossey-Bass, 2011), 62–63, italics in the original.

10. Rob Bell, *What Is the Bible?* (San Francisco: HarperOne, 2017), 271. Italicized words are emphasized in the original.

11. Nadia Bolz-Weber, *Shameless: A Sexual Reformation* (Crown Publishing Group, 2019), 13.

12. Bolz-Weber, *Shameless*, 72.

13. Richard Rohr, *The Divine Dance* (New Kensington, PA: Whitaker House, 2016), Kindle loc. 2827–28.

14. Andrew Wilson, *Unbreakable: What the Son of God Said about the Word of God* (La Grange, KY: 10Publishing, 2015), Kindle loc. 142–43.

15. Matthew 22:43, NIV, emphasis mine.

16. Michael J. Kruger, "Is the Church over the Bible or Is the Bible over the Church?," Canon Fodder, October 6, 2014, https://www.michaeljkruger .com/there-is-no-bible-in-the-bible-really/.

17. John Wenham, *Christ and the Bible*, 3rd ed. (Eugene, OR: Wipf & Stock, 2009), 28.

18. See Michael J. Kruger, *The Question of Canon: Challenging the Status Quo in the New Testament Church* (Downers Grove, IL: IVP, 2013).

19. Pete Enns, "I Love You, Bible . . . Just Not That Way," blog post, https://peteenns.com/i-love-the-bible/.

20. Brian McLaren, *A New Kind of Christianity* (San Francisco: HarperOne, 2010), 80.

21. McLaren, *A New Kind of Christianity*, 78.

22. McLaren, *A New Kind of Christianity*, 79.

23. G. K. Chesterton, *The Autobiography of G. K. Chesterton* (San Francisco: Ignatius Press, 2006), 217.

CHAPTER 10: HELL ON EARTH?

1. Rob Bell, *Love Wins* (San Francisco: HarperOne, 2011), 81.

2. Bell, *Love Wins*, vi.

3. Brian Zahnd, *Sinners in the Hands of a Loving God* (New York: Crown Publishing Group, 2017), 126.

4. Richard Rohr, "A Toxic Image of God," Center for Action and Contemplation, January 28, 2016, https://cac.org/a-toxic-image-of-god-2016-01-28/.

5. William Paul Young, *Lies We Believe about God* (New York: Atria Books, 2017), 118.

6. Jesse James DeConto, "For All the Sinners and Saints: An Interview with Nadia Bolz-Weber," *Religion & Politics*, July 28, 2015, https://religionandpolitics.org/2015/07/28/for-all-the-sinners-and-saints-an-interview-with-nadia-bolz-weber/.

7. Michael McClymond, "How Universalism, 'the Opiate of the Theologians,' Went Mainstream," interview by Paul Copan, *Christianity Today*, March 11, 2019, https://www.christianitytoday.com/ct/2019/march-web-only/michael-mcclymond-devils-redemption-universalism.html.

8. Richard Bauckham, "Universalism: A Historical Survey," *Themelios* 4, no. 2 (September 1978): 47–48, https://www.theologicalstudies.org.uk/article_universalism_bauckham.html.

9. Richard Rohr, "A Toxic Image of God."

10. Richard Rohr, "A Toxic Image of God."

11. Norman Geisler and Thomas Howe, *When Critics Ask: A Popular Handbook on Bible Difficulties* (Wheaton, IL.: Victor Books, 1992).

12. J. I. Packer, "What Is Hell?" *100 Huntley*, April 21, 2009, YouTube video, 2:37, https://www.youtube.com/watch?v=rMyWd4rTMD0.

13. J. I. Packer, "What Is Hell?"

14. See, for example, Francis Chan and Preston Sprinkle, *Erasing Hell: What*

God Said about Eternity, and the Things We've Made Up (Colorado Springs: David C. Cook, 2011), 52.

15. C. S. Lewis, *The Problem of Pain* (San Francisco: Harper One, 2009), 127.

CHAPTER 11: COSMIC CHILD ABUSE?

1. Tony Jones, *Did God Kill Jesus? Searching for Love in History's Most Famous Execution* (San Francisco: HarperOne, 2015), part 4.

2. Larry Getlen, "This Man Wrote a Small Book for His Family—and It Became a Best-Seller," *New York Post*, December 25, 2016, https://nypost.com/2016/12/25/this-man-wrote-a-small-book-for-his-family-and-it-became-a-best-seller/.

3. William Paul Young, *The Shack* (Newbury Park, CA: Windblown Media, 2007), 210, Kindle.

4. William Paul Young, *Lies We Believe about God* (New York: Atria Books, 2017), 149–51.

5. Young, *Lies We Believe about God*, 169.

6. See Justin Taylor, "Response to Wright from the Authors of 'Pierced for Our Transgressions,'" Gospel Coalition blog, April 24, 2007, https://www.thegospelcoalition.org/blogs/justin-taylor/response-to-wright-from-authors-of/. Chalke's statement originally appeared in his article "Cross Purposes," *Christianity* magazine, September 2004, 44–48.

7. Rob Bell, *What Is the Bible?* (San Francisco: HarperOne, 2017), 244.

8. Bell, *What Is the Bible?*, 245.

9. Brian Zahnd, *Sinners in the Hands of a Loving God* (New York: Crown Publishing Group, 2017), 86.

10. Brian Zahnd, "Monster God or Monster Man," (debate between Zahnd and Michael Brown), International House of Prayer Symposium, September 13, 2014), YouTube video, 14:54, https://www.youtube.com/watch?v=aGYFjKa5n0Y.

11. Richard Rohr, "Jesus and the Cross: Changing Perspectives," Center for Action and Contemplation, February 5, 2019, https://cac.org/changing-perspectives-2019-02-05/.

12. Bell, *What Is the Bible?*, 244–45.

13. Zahnd, *Sinners in the Hands of a Loving God*, 86.

14. See Albert Mohler, "Has the Message of Jesus Been Lost?" AlbertMohler.com, April 27, 2005, https://albertmohler.com/2005/04/27/has-the-message-of-jesus-been-lost/.

15. Richard Rohr, "Jesus and the Cross: Substitutionary Atonement," Center for Action and Contemplation, February 3, 2019, https://cac.org/substitutionary-atonement-2019-02-03/.

16. Richard Rohr, "New Orthodoxy in Light of Emerging Faith," YouTube,

January 17, 2015, https://www.youtube.com/watch?v=dHTty9l6Btw (8:40).

17. Rachel Held Evans, *Inspired: Slaying Giants, Walking on Water, and Loving the Bible Again* (Nashville: Thomas Nelson, 2018), 154.

18. Zahnd, *Sinners in the Hands of a Loving God*, 86–87.

19. Brian D. McLaren, *Why Did Jesus, Moses, the Buddha, and Mohammed Cross the Road?* (New York: Jericho Books, 2012), 212.

20. Zahnd, *Sinners in the Hands of a Loving God*, 86.

21. Jay Sklar, *Leviticus: An Introduction and Commentary* (Downers Grove, IL: IVP Academic, 2014), 42.

22. Miroslav Volf, *Free of Charge: Giving and Forgiving in a Culture Stripped of Grace* (Grand Rapids, MI: Zondervan, 2005), 138–39.

23. R. Scott Smith, *Authentically Emergent: In Search of a Truly Progressive Christianity* (Eugene, OR: Cascade Books, 2018), 160–161.

24. Mark Mittelberg, *The Reason Why Faith Makes Sense* (Carol Stream, IL: Tyndale, 2001), 78.

CHAPTER 12: RECONSTRUCTION

1. Or listen to his own summary in this lecture: "The Essentials of the Faith," Education Underground, June 17, 2013, YouTube video, 52:29, https://www.youtube.com/watch?v=pjdy-VWXrik.

2. See Romans 3:23; 1 Timothy 2:5; Ephesians 2:8-9; Romans 10:9; 1 John 4:2; John 3:16; 1 Corinthians 15:12; Acts 16:31; Hebrews 11:6.

3. See "The Chicago Statement on Biblical Inerrancy," Article XIX, at https://www.etsjets.org/files/documents/Chicago_Statement.pdf. For more on the history and background of this statement, see John Stonestreet, "Chicago Statement on Biblical Inerrancy an Evangelical Milestone," *The Pathway*, January 18, 2019, https://mbcpathway.com/2019/01/18/chicago-statement-on-biblical-inerrancy-an-evangelical-milestone/.

4. Dietrich Bonhoeffer, *The Cost of Discipleship* (New York: Touchstone, 1995), 44–45.

5. Eric Metaxas, *Bonhoeffer: Pastor, Martyr, Prophet, Spy* (Nashville: Thomas Nelson), 528.

6. "The Hitchens Transcript," *Portland Monthly*, January 2010, https://www.pdxmonthly.com/news-and-city-life/2009/12/christopher-hitchens.

7. Revelation 5:12-13